"*Change at the Core* provides insight for those leading a strategic change initiative—with emphasis on winning the hearts and enthusiasm of the individuals who will bring their capabilities to bear to make the change a reality."

~ Alan A. Malinchak
Vice President/Chief Learning Officer ManTech International

"The authors take on an important and timeless topic—powering change—in pragmatic terms. This field guide provides practical tools that help leaders to unleash individual commitment and close the change gap."

~ John Malitoris
Regional Managing Director, Duke Corporate Education

"A helpful book for anyone tasked with leading change from the middle of their organization. Filled with practical advice for involving team members and generating individual commitment."

~ Rick Maurer
Author, *Leading from the Middle*

"I thoroughly enjoyed reading *Change at the Core*. It was right on target in identifying that Style, Passion and Mindset influence each person's acceptance of change. The real world examples put the concepts covered in proper perspective. I will be certain to include what I learned from this book in my Project Management and Information Technology courses."

~ Dr. Nabil Bedewi, PMP
Visiting Assistant Professor
McDonough School of Business, Georgetown University

D1310218

CHANGE
at the CORE

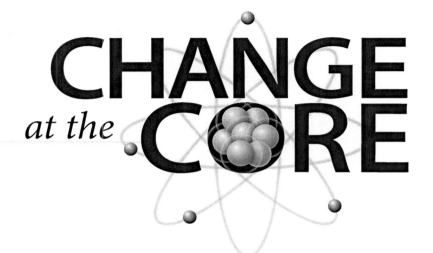

CHANGE
at the CORE

Unleash Your Team's
Energy to Drive Results

PEAK
PUBLISHING

Woodland Park, Colorado

CHANGE at the CORE

Unleash Your Team's Energy to Drive Results

By Wendy Mack and Myron Radio

Peak Publishing

P.O. Box 5980

Woodland Park, CO 80866-5980

(719) 687-8561

info@peakpublishing.org

To order this book, visit www.ChangeAtTheCore.com

ISBN 978-0-9819517-0-6

Library of Congress Control Number: 2009900461

Copy editor: Amy Mayer

Cover design and layout: Steffi Rubin

First Printing: March 2009

Table of Contents

Why Change Leadership is More Crucial than Ever

Whether you are a director, vice-president, functional leader, or program or project lead, one of the most powerful and pivotal roles you can play in your organization is that of a change leader.

Markets change, technologies evolve, the competition shifts, and mergers and acquisitions occur. As a result, your organization must constantly change in order to succeed and survive. And it is your job to lead the transformation.

The Challenge of Being a Change Leader

You know that changing will help your organization gain a competitive advantage, enter new markets, improve the productivity and effectiveness of your workforce, and so on. Yet, when your employees hear about a new change effort, most will shudder and roll their eyes. In fact, when we interviewed leaders about change efforts, they repeatedly cited resistance as the primary obstacle to transformation. We heard countless stories like the two below.

> "Our executive team had a vision of becoming an end-to-end service provider for government IT projects. Rather than trying to get there through organic growth, we have been aggressively acquiring smaller competitors to round out our portfolio. We've acquired eight companies in just over three years. On paper, we look good. We've managed to get everyone migrated over to the same ERP, e-mail servers, and performance management systems. In reality though, it's a complete mess. We are still operating like nine different companies. The leaders from each of

Why is change so painful for so many? One reason is that changes are typically dictated from the top and are imposed on people rather than implemented with them.

the acquired companies refuse to take any action that doesn't serve the interests of their group first. At leadership meetings, everyone pretends to agree with the integrated strategy. But as soon as they are out of the room, they compete with each other. Our customers have been complaining that we sometimes have three salespeople calling them. They think our left hand doesn't know what our right is doing."

~ Senior Manager, Aerospace Industry

"Our agency used to be organized by the target groups that we serve. We had separate units responsible for elder care, foster children, people with disabilities, and so on. Over time, we came to realize that while our staff was doing their very best, people were falling through the cracks. Earlier this year, we moved to an integrated approach, where we assigned each family one case worker. The case worker would have overall responsibility for helping that family with all of the issues associated with navigating public services. Each case worker is supposed to work with specialists as needed. We thought that employees would be excited about the reorganization because it is clearly better for our clients. Instead they are resisting the change at every step of the way."

~ Managing Director, Public Service Agency

Why is change so painful for so many? One reason is that changes are typically dictated from the top and are imposed on people rather than implemented with them. At the same time, changes often occur simultaneously—with one change initiative overlapping and/or overtaking another. Employees at all levels begin to suffer from fatigue and frustration. In many cases, people feel victimized by change. They might ask:

- Who decided this?

- What are "they" doing to "us" now?

- How can we possibly do everything that needs to be done all at once?

- Don't they know we have our day jobs too?

This often leads to sentiments like:

- I feel manipulated and mismanaged.

- I hate it here.

- This stinks.

- I can't wait to get out of here.

How can you preemptively address negative emotions? How can you proactively engage, empower, and align your people for joint success?

The answer is Change at the Core.

These are the very last thoughts and emotions you want your people to experience! In today's knowledge-based economy, your people are your most critical resources. People are the lifeblood of your organization. The last thing you want to do is cause doubt, disengagement, and cynicism among the very people you are counting on to be customer-focused, innovative, creative, and productive!

So, how can you preemptively address negative emotions? How can you proactively engage, empower, and align your people for joint success? How can you engage your employees to volunteer for change initiatives at the grassroots level? Where can you turn when you don't know where to begin? The answer is learning to lead *Change at the Core.*

Change at the Core is a process for leading change that focuses on the individuals at every level of your organization.

What is Change at the Core?

Change at the Core is a process for leading change that focuses on the individuals at every level of your organization. The process merges overall best practices in change management with recent developments in assessment methodologies to provide a powerful new approach for leaders at all levels.

Thanks to these new developments, we can actually predict with great certainty how individuals will react and adapt to change. By being able to predict those reactions, leaders can create implementation strategies that not only reduce resistance, but that actually create a firestorm of support.

Change at the Core is grounded in the belief that the most effective way to get people to embrace and accelerate change is to unleash the energy that is at the core of each person. It is not a magic bullet, but it is a crucial tool for anyone who strives to be an effective change leader.

How to Use this Book

This book is both an introduction to a new perspective on change management and a practical field guide. We suggest that you first read the book in its entirety and then come back to specific sections and chapters to delve more deeply into the areas that most interest you. The worksheets and activities will help you translate the general concepts into specific actions you can implement with your own team.

- **Section 1** presents the need for a new perspective and introduces you to the process you will learn in later chapters.

- **Section 2** goes into depth about internal energy—a concept that is critical to understand in order to apply the Change at the Core process.

- **Section 3** provides the details of the Change at the Core process and tips and techniques for mastering each step of the process.

- **Section 4** offers practical advice for putting everything you have learned to work in order to launch and sustain change initiatives.

Will You Rise to the Challenge?

Organizations of all sizes in all sectors need more people at every level who can lead the human side of change. They need leaders who can:

- Communicate a vision;

- inspire people to take action;

- engage stakeholders;

- respond to resistance; and

- deliver results.

Many of the leaders we've met report that their proudest accomplishments revolve around a time that they led a change successfully and accomplished it through a total team effort.

In fact, in their bestselling book, *The Leadership Challenge*, Jim Kouzes and Barry Posner suggest that the study of leadership is in fact "the study of how men and women guide us through adversity, uncertainty, hardship, disruption, transformation, and transition."[1] In other words, leadership is all about change and change requires leadership.

Up until now, you may have dreaded being assigned to transformation teams. If so, you've probably been the victim of poorly planned and badly implemented change programs. You have had firsthand experience with the common problems that plague change efforts. You know that research shows that up to 70 percent of change efforts fail.[2] Who would want all of the stress and headaches? If that's the case, this book is for you. After learning our model

Many leaders report that their proudest accomplishments revolve around a time that they led a change successfully and accomplished it through a total team effort.

Internal energy is one competitive advantage that has been largely untapped.

for leading change at the core, you will be equipped to tackle these problems and guide your team and organization to success.

On the other hand, you may be a natural change leader—someone who thrives on complex challenges and who understands both the people and process sides of any transformation project. If that sounds like you, this book is for you too! You recognize that since change is complex, you need to continually learn more tools, techniques, and approaches that will enhance your ability to address and resolve challenges. You are constantly on the lookout for approaches that will help you lead your team to better, faster results. As you read about Change at the Core, you will discover that internal energy is a competitive advantage that has been largely untapped.

In either case—read on! You'll be glad you did.

SECTION ONE

A New Lens on Leading Change

"It's not the strongest of the species that survives,
nor the most intelligent.
It is the one that is most adaptable to change."
~ Charles Darwin

1

The Need for a New Lens

Existing Advice on Leading Change

Harvard professor John Kotter put it best when he said, "We live in an age when change is accelerating."[3] Unfortunately, most organizations are not fully prepared to respond to constant change. According to a recent study sponsored by IBM, a rising number of CEOs are concerned about their organizations' ability to manage change.[4]

The macro perspective alone is not enough.

While scores of books have been written on the topic of leading change, we believe there is a significant gap in the existing advice on the topic. Most books focus on change from a *macro* perspective. They are written for THE LEADER of an organization—the person with both a particular vision and the power to implement it. A review of the most respected books in this genre shows that there are common and consistent themes when it comes to best practices for leading organization-wide change.[5]

Best Practices for Leading Change: The Macro Perspective

1. Convey a sense of urgency.

2. Focus the organization around a vision.

3. Engage stakeholders to ensure alignment.

4. Communicate constantly.

5. Dedicate yourself to maintaining momentum

We don't doubt the advice of these experts and would, in fact, highly recommend a number of specific books to anyone looking for guidance about how to lead organization-wide change. However, we believe that the macro perspective alone is not enough. Consider the case study below.

What Went Wrong?

A few years ago, two giants in the advertising industry merged. For the sake of confidentiality, let's call them Agency A and Agency B. Executives from both agencies worked with an outside consulting firm for more than nine months to plan the merger. Many arguments, much analysis, and months of planning led to final agreement on the terms of the merger. The board decided that the new organization would be called AB Advertising and they chose the CEO of Agency A to head the new company.

Once the merger was announced and a new organizational structure was put into place, the new CEO created an Integration Management Office. The IMO team consisted of the newly appointed COO for AB Advertising as well as the heads of each of the various functions including Sales, IT, Marketing, Product Development, Legal and Regulatory, Communications, and Human Resources.

In this example, the CEO and the COO were ultimately responsible for the overall success of the merger. They partnered with an outside consulting firm to plan and oversee the alignment of all of the systems and processes. The Chief Human Capital Officer worked closely with the CEO and COO to address issues such as organizational design, integrating cultures, and employee communication. They followed and benefited from the advice of change experts.

Unfortunately, despite the expertise within and available to this executive team, the merger was a failure. AB Advertising's stock price fell from $32/share to just under $3/share in two years. Many of the most talented people quit within the first nine months. Those who remained were disillusioned and disengaged.

While the executives in our example did many things right from a *macro* perspective, a closer analysis revealed that there were many failures and break-downs within each functional area. Many leaders from key departments had never led a significant transition and failed to understand, engage, and align the *people* who would actually drive real change.

The people we are talking about are at the core of any organization. They aren't leaders in the traditional sense of the word. They are the frontline employees, technical leads, and supervisors who make up 80 to 90 percent of your staff. Many leaders think of this group as being "recipients" of change rather than "drivers" of change. In reality, the people on the front line are imperative to any change effort.

Some experts talk about getting people "on board" with change. To us, the concept of getting people on board sets up the wrong visual image. As a leader, you don't want people who are along for the ride. You want every individual in your organization to be doing everything within his/her power to make the change successful. In fact, we like to picture every employee as being drivers themselves. Rather than sitting back and looking at the scenery, each person is making daily decisions about how fast to drive, where to turn, and whether to break or bend the rules.

Let's look at two specific examples from AB Advertising that illustrate what happens when leaders have the mindset of getting employees to "get on board" with change rather than a mindset focused on engaging employees to drive change themselves.

> Dan is the VP of Sales for AB Advertising. When the merger was announced, Dan was quick to step up and make the case that he should head the integrated sales team. He immediately saw the potential in the merger of two top-notch sales teams and he was excited about leading the effort to double his company's revenue.
>
> Unfortunately for Dan, the people inside the sales organization were not as quick to get on board. Every time he met with the group,

As a leader, you don't want people who are along for the ride. You want every individual in your organization to be doing everything within his/her power to make the change successful.

19

they complained about not knowing enough about the new offerings to be able to sell successfully. A number of sales people were complaining that their territories now overlapped and that clients were getting duplicate calls. Several others said that the new sales tracking tool they were supposed to use was cumbersome and slow. After the first year, instead of doubling sales, the team barely managed to close enough deals to keep the company afloat.

Dan tried pushing the team. He threatened individuals with the prospect of losing their jobs. When people expressed reservations or brought up barriers he told them to "get on the bus or get off." Instead of feeling motivated, the team felt deflated and the resistance simply went underground. People stopped participating in meetings and raising issues. A few people quit. Everyone else just kept his/her head down in an attempt to avoid Dan's wrath. Nothing improved.

Chris headed up the Human Capital Team for AB Advertising during the merger. For a period of about 18 months, Chris was responsible for leading a team of human resources professionals who were tasked with integrating all of the talent management functions across the merged companies.

Shortly after accepting the assignment, Chris was told that the executives wanted to move everyone to the performance management and compensation planning system that had been in place at Agency A. Unfortunately, Agency B had spent two years and hundreds of thousands of dollars rolling out a different system just before the merger. Several people on Chris's team were upset. Everyone dreaded having to convince managers and employees that this was the best approach. Chris tried pleading with her team. She let them know that they didn't have a choice and that they "had to make the best of it." She divided up the work that needed to be done and established key milestones.

People did the minimum that they could to get by. When people brought up the resistance they were hearing from managers and attempted to ask questions, she told them there was not much that could be done because "this is what management wants." Team meetings were dismal. In the first year, compliance with the new system was below 60 percent and employee satisfaction scores concerning pay and performance plummeted.

So were Dan and Chris at fault for the failure of the merger? No. Similar scenarios were being played out across every team, unit, and division that made up AB Advertising. Although the company executives had a clear reason for merging and a vision for the future, Dan, Chris, and the other individual leaders throughout the organization never received the tools and training they needed help their own people embrace and accelerate change.

In the case of AB Advertising, the executives who planned the merger probably pictured a top-notch sales force that would be happy to join forces with a past competitor and would be aggressive about promoting new products and services. The executives who decided on the compensation and performance management system certainly had reasons for their choice and expected others to recognize the benefits as well. As we saw, it didn't work out that way.

We call this breakdown between the top of the organization and the front line the Change Gap.

The Change Gap

Change gaps are common and pervasive. In its simplest form, a change gap can be thought of as the difference between what a leader is picturing (the vision for the future) and what people are actually doing.

Leaders need to be able to close the change gap.

The vision a leader has for the organization

What people are actually doing

Change gaps occur for many reasons. Here are a few of the most common causes:

- What matters to executives is different from what matters to the front line.

- Executives speak in financial terms while the majority of the organization is used to speaking in technical terms.

- Executives are paid to position their organizations for the future, while managers, supervisors, and frontline employees are rewarded for getting things done within the present system.

- Top leaders speak in terms of strategy while the rest of the organization is focused on the tactical.

In order to lead change successfully, leaders need to be able to close the change gap.

Real-World Challenges

Unfortunately, closing the change gap is not easy. Much of the existing advice on change assumes that the people who are leading a change are the same people who conceived of it in the first place. Unless you work in a very small organization, that is usually not the case. Think about your own experience with leading change projects. How often were you the originator of the idea?

In the real world, change is often initiated at one level and then passed on to another person or group. This person or group then needs to influence another person or group to take ownership, and so on.

In an Ideal World	In the Real World
The people responsible for implementing change would be part of the planning team that chooses the solution.	Change efforts are often launched when specific solutions are mandated from the top of the organization.
The people affected by a change would have direct and personal input.	People have to accept and live with changes that they did not influence.

While the idea that change will "trickle down" through an organization seems to make sense in theory, in the real world it rarely happens that way. The reality is that change is not linear. It's messy and complex. And as a change is cascaded through an organization, the change gap often widens because the people who are being counted on to close the gap may lack understanding, acceptance, and buy-in themselves. As a result, change efforts tend to fall apart over time rather than gain steam.

What's the Solution?

Whether an organization is made up of 500, 5,000, or 50,000 people, change only happens when individuals are motivated to take action and to do things differently.

According to systems expert, Margaret Wheatley, "Large scale changes that have the greatest impact do not originate in plans or strategies from on high. Instead, they begin as small, local actions.…What you can do is begin to create system-wide change by working locally where you learn to be the change you want to see.…Your work is to encourage local experiments, to nourish supportive beliefs and dynamics, and to sponsor people to connect with all the kindred spirits now working in isolation."[6]

Instead of attempting to drive change throughout an entire organization all at once, we believe that change champions should focus first on influencing and connecting with the specific individuals on their team.

Individual Commitment

As management consultant Connie Hritz says, "If you've lived through change, you already know that it occurs one person at a time…so focus your change management efforts on getting individual commitment."[7]

Getting individual commitment is at the heart of our Change at the Core process. As each leader connects with his/her own team using this process, the focus is on truly engaging the heads, hearts, and hands of each person.

If Dan, Chris, and the other leaders from AB Advertising had connected, communicated, and collaborated with each of their key people in a way that generated commitment, the merger might have turned out differently. Dan and Chris would have focused their efforts on gaining individual buy-in, support, and commitment. Once their people had taken true, deep ownership of change, these individuals would have become change leaders themselves.

By teaching Change at the Core, we've helped scores of leaders close change gaps and lead change efforts successfully—even when they and their teams weren't the originators of the change.

Chapter Highlights

Employees at all levels are actually in the driver's seat when it comes to making change a reality. For a change to be rolled out successfully across an organization, each and every leader needs to translate the change so that it makes sense and is meaningful for the individuals on his/her team.

Change only happens when individuals are motivated to take action and to do things differently.

"Never doubt that a small group of committed individuals

can change the world—

in fact that is all that ever has."

~ Margaret Mead, American Cultural Anthropologist

*Individual commitment
is at the heart of the
Change at the Core
process.*

2

Introducing Change at the Core

The Connection between Energy and Change

Organization researchers are discovering what you may already know intuitively—energy plays a critical role in individual, team, and organizational performance. As leadership expert Richard Neslund puts it, "Energy is the fuel that powers the engines of performance."[8]

All change requires energy.

> Picture the last time you were in a big airport—Denver maybe. All throughout the concourse are long, moving walkways. What do some people do when they get to a moving walkway? THEY STOP WALKING! They just kind of lean back, and wait for the sidewalk to get them to their destination. What about the people in your organization? Are they sitting back and waiting for someone else to get them there? Or do they have the energy, motivation, and drive to take action and move forward themselves?

When it comes to leading change, energy becomes even more imperative. In 2008, the global management consulting firm McKinsey & Company surveyed 1,500 executives about transformation projects. McKinsey found that the companies whose change efforts were successful reported that they had been able to sustain and mobilize organizational energy during the transformation. The same survey showed that more than half of the companies with failed change efforts reported that they were unsuccessful at mobilizing and sustaining energy.[9]

How Do You Generate Energy?

The key to leading change starts with your ability to energize others.

Consider this: Researchers from IBM's Institute for Knowledge-Based Management, the University of Michigan, and the University of Virginia collaboratively studied the flow of energy in the workplace and found that people who are "energizers":

- Are more likely to have their ideas considered and put into action;

- get more input, information, and commitment from those around them; and

- attract the commitment of other high performers.

In addition, people who worked with and around energizers tended to perform better than those who worked with or around de-energizers.[10]

Being an energizer is not about "projecting" energy as much as it about uncovering and unleashing energy to achieve a specific result.

Being an energizing leader is not about delivering motivational speeches and holding pizza parties at work. While the ability to inspire is important, effective leaders recognize that being an energizer is not about "projecting" energy as much as it about uncovering and unleashing energy to achieve a specific result.

Sources of Energy

So where does energy come from? Through our research and hands-on experience with clients, we discovered that there are four sources of energy at work inside organizations:

1. Individual team members' style, passion, and mindset (Internal Energy)

2. Productive interpersonal and small group conversations (Interpersonal Energy)

3. Alignment at the team or unit level around values, goals, and approaches (Group Energy)

4. A shared sense of urgency and commitment to action across the organization (Organizational Energy)

Sources of Energy at Work	Keys to Uncovering and Unleashing this Energy
Internal Energy	Tapping into each Individual's… • Style • Passion • Mindset
Interpersonal Energy[11]	Interactions… • In which a compelling vision is created • To which each person can contribute meaningfully • With others who are fully engaged and participating • Which are marked by progress • When hope becomes part of the equation
Group Energy[12]	Teams or Units that have… • An "igniting" purpose • Cooperative mindsets • Seamless boundaries • The capacity to produce results
Organizational Energy	Employees at all levels share… • A sense of urgency • A clear sense of direction • A commitment to action • Empowerment

Organizational Energy

Much of the literature available on leading and communicating change focuses on organizational energy. Organizational energy occurs when employees at all levels share a sense of urgency, a clear sense of direction, a commitment to action, and empowerment.

Of course no one would deny that change is more successful when there is organizational energy. Unfortunately, too many leaders rely on the wrong methods in their attempts to reach this point. They want to hold town hall meetings that energize 20,000 people in one fell swoop. What typically ends up happening is that people feel a temporary surge during a meeting like this, but not enough individual commitment to implement lasting changes in behavior. We have found that organizational energy is truly achieved only when corporate and mass communication methods are combined with the actions of individual leaders who leverage internal, interpersonal, and group energy.

Interpersonal energy combined with good management results in group energy.

Interpersonal and Group Energy

Group and interpersonal energy are closely linked. Interpersonal energy comes from the interactions that take place between individual employees and their colleagues and managers. When interpersonal energy is combined with the fundamentals of good management (a clear purpose, effective processes, conflict resolution, and removal of barriers) the result is group energy.

Without a doubt, interpersonal and group energy are crucial for successful change. Yet again though, neither can be achieved without first attending to the most personal and powerful aspect of energy—internal energy.

As the box on the previous page shows, interpersonal energy requires each person to be able to contribute meaningfully. It also arises as a result of a compelling vision. Two key factors in group energy are an igniting purpose and cooperative mindsets. A crucial perspective of this book is that all of these elements—meaningful contribution, compelling vision, igniting purpose, and mindset—are, in fact, highly personal.

Making a meaningful contribution may mean something different for you than it does for your colleague next door. A vision might be compelling for one person yet remain unconvincing to another person. The purpose that ignites me may do little to motivate you.

To create the energy for change, we need to be able to tap into the highly personal and unique internal energy at the core of each and every person.

Internal Energy

This book focuses on internal energy for two reasons. First, as we discussed in Chapter 1, no change takes place without individual changes in behavior. For your change effort to be a success, you need each person on your team to be motivated to take proactive steps to do something differently. They need to be energized enough to overcome inertia, habits, and the status quo.

Second, we have discovered that internal energy is a powerful source of motivation. Tapping into a person's internal energy is like tapping into a gusher of oil. When you understand what drives each person on your team, your job becomes easy. You don't need to micromanage your team—you unleash and channel your team members' energy and get out of the way!

Internal energy is the most powerful source of motivation.

Essentials of Change at the Core

Change at the Core is about powering change from within. The source of that power is the internal energy that is at the core of every person you work with.

In Section 3 of this book you will learn a step-by-step process for leading Change at the Core. The key actions to remember for now are to:

1. Understand each person's internal energy.

2. Connect and communicate to promote openness to change.

3. Understand, appreciate, and address resistance.

4. Align and unleash each person's energy to power the change.

Your most effective tool for leading change is leveraging the energy at the core of each person.

Chapter Highlights

Your most effective tool for leading change is leveraging the energy at the core of each person. The ability to do this well is the focus of this book.

Before you read more about each step in detail, review Section 2 to learn the essentials of internal energy.

SECTION TWO

Understanding Internal Energy:
Style, Passion, and Mindset

"Constituents want visions of the future that reflect their own aspirations.
They want to hear how their dreams will come true
and their hopes will be fulfilled."
~ James Kouzes and Barry Posner

3

What is Internal Energy?

This section covers the elements of internal energy. Before you read on, reflect on these questions.

What if you had a way to identify what motivates each person on your team?

- What do the words "motivation" and "energized" mean to you?

- How do you recognize when someone is motivated and energized?

- Would knowing someone's motivation be important to you?

Motivation Magic

Employee motivation is a perennial hot topic for leaders at all levels. Hundreds of thousands of books on motivational methods and tools are purchased every year. Advice on motivation covers topics ranging from the design of pay systems to creating a great place to work to giving people time off. None of this advice is wrong, but none of it is right either. Motivation is highly personal and largely internal. What matters to one person may mean nothing to his or her colleagues.

What if you had a way to identify what motivates each person on your team? What if your conversations with each employee could be tailored to emphasize what matters most to him or her? What if you could match each person's tasks and overall responsibilities to his or her strengths? You can do all of this if you understand internal energy.

What is Internal Energy?

Internal energy is the combined force of each person's:

- Style

- Passion

- Mindset

The following chapters will explain each of the three elements in detail. For now, let's use some basic definitions:

Style	HOW we do what we do
Passion	WHY we do what we do
Mindset	WHAT we focus on

Examples of Internal Energy at Work

Let's look at few examples of how an individual's internal energy drives his or her behavior.

Style

Remember Dan from the AB Advertising example in Chapter 1? Dan had a style that was very forceful and aggressive. Dan was energized by moving fast and getting results. He attempted to push his sales team to accept the changes and get on with doing their jobs. While there are times that this style can be effective, the early stages of a major transformation require a much different approach. Dan needed to learn to adapt his style to show support for his people and genuine interest in their concerns.

Passion

Ed was tasked with evaluating and redesigning his company's leadership training programs. Ed couldn't wait to get started. He bought or borrowed every book ever written on the topics of leadership and leadership development. He spent six months developing an instrument to gather input from leaders about their own training needs. When the data came in, Ed took another four months to analyze the input and integrate it with what he'd learned from the literature. With two months left in the calendar year, Ed was hard at work developing a model that would integrate all of the possible training programs that the company could offer. Not a single course had been designed or piloted. Ed was shocked when his manager exploded and demanded that the entire new curriculum be ready by the end of the year.

What Ed's manager didn't realize is that Ed has a passion for knowledge. He was highly energized by learning and developing theories and he had been happy during all of those months that the manager felt were wasted. If Ed and his manager had understood each other's motivations (passions) and had been able to talk about one another's priorities, they may have been come up with an approach that was both rigorous and that resulted in a faster redesign.

Mindset

Connie led a team that was in charge of rolling out a new performance management and compensation system. As it turned out, all of the members of Connie's project team were focused on the process side of the work. They created detailed project plans and step-by-step process descriptions. Despite the team's brilliant work on the processes, the people in the organization ended up resisting the changes. Why? Because no one on Connie's team had made plans for generating commitment, support, and acceptance. As a team, they lacked a deliberate focus on the people side of the transformation.

The Connection to Head, Heart, Hands

How many times have you heard someone say?

"She doesn't have her head in the game."

"His heart is not in it."

"His behavior is getting out of hand."

At some level, we all know that an individual's performance is impacted by his/her head, heart, and hands. Not surprisingly, change consultants and researchers have discovered that the head/heart/hands metaphor is helpful when it comes to learning to lead change. Leaders are often taught that they need to:

1. Influence people's heads—showing the rational, logical reasons for a change.

2. Connect to people's hearts—helping them feel a need for change.

3. Focus on people's hands—giving them the tools they need to effect change.

We certainly find this advice to be helpful when creating communication plans and engagement events for large groups of people. However, the true power of heads, hearts, and hands is diluted when we only use it with the lens of mass communication and training.

We have found that a much more powerful approach lies in the ability of change leaders to understand and connect with each *individual's* head, heart, and hands. Understanding style, passion, and mindset allows you to do just that.

The true power of heads, hearts, and hands is diluted when we only use it with the lens of mass communication and training.

Dan's hands were dedicated to getting things done. He used a *Driving Style*. (See Chapter 4 for more on styles.)

Ed's heart was in learning about leadership development. He had a *Passion for Knowledge*. (See Chapter 5 for more on passions.)

Connie's project team had their heads focused on processes. They had a *Process Mindset*. (See Chapter 6 for more on mindsets.)

Internal Energy Element	*Each person's...*
Style	Hands
Passion	Heart
Mindset	Head

Visualizing Internal Energy

We picture the interaction of the three elements much like the layers of planet earth.

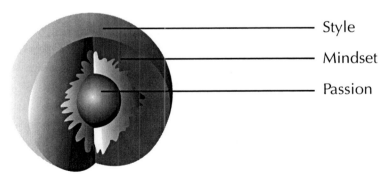

Style

Mindset

Passion

As this diagram illustrates, our passion is at the very center of our core. Just as the core of the earth is a fiery mass, our passion is the core of who we are.

Our mindset is like the middle layer of the earth—fluid, changeable, and greatly impacted by the passion at our core. While our passion gives us energy, our mindset determines where our energy is focused.

Finally, our style is the outermost layer. It's the first thing people see when they interact with us. Just as the earth model shows, style is only on the surface.

Measuring Style, Passion, and Mindset

Throughout this book we will talk about style, passion, and mindset in that order. Our reason for doing so is that style is the most noticeable, observable element of internal energy. Passions are harder to observe, but with true effort and open conversations you can begin to gauge a person's passions. Mindset is what is happening in our heads. As such, it is extremely difficult to determine another person's mindset.

In our work with teams over the past three decades, we have utilized a variety of assessment tools that measure people's preferred behavior style. These assessments allow observers to place people into several different categories in an effort to explain and predict their behaviors or actions. Generally, we find that an understanding of styles helps team members appreciate one another and adapt to people with different styles.

Over time, we added additional assessments to our portfolios. Two of these assessments gauged what people couldn't readily discern from simply observing behavior. The assessment for mindsets helped us understand what a particular individual is focused on—his mindset or what he holds in his head. The other assessment helped individuals identify her motivations or passions—what she held in her heart.

We discovered that the real power in using all of these tools lies in the implications about where we get our internal energy and understanding that the things that energize us in turn drive our behavior. Rather than simply understanding and accepting how each person behaves (his or her style) we could now connect with what people were focusing on and why.

Now, for the first time, we are able to map a person's work activities to his/her energy patterns and leverage resources across the team for greater joint success. Imagine the impact this can have on the productivity of your workforce!

For the first time, we are able to map a person's work activities to his/her energy patterns and leverage resources across the team for greater joint success.

Leveraging Internal Energy to Lead Change

What if Dan had recognized that his aggressive style was causing his team to feel steamrolled? He may have been able to shift to a style that was more supportive during the emotional phase of the transition. When his people felt more supported, as their questions were answered, and as the kinks in the system were worked out, he could have shifted back to driving results.

What if Ed's manager had recognized that Ed was energized by learning while he himself was energized by producing results? They could have explicitly discussed ways to satisfy both passions. Perhaps they could have agreed to pilot a new course within the first six months. Maybe Ed could have viewed the pilot as an opportunity to learn.

What if Connie had recognized that her project team members' heads were all focused on processes? She could have tapped a person or a subset of the team to focus on the people side of the transformation.

Chapter Highlights

Internal energy is the combined force of each person's:

- Style

- Passion

- Mindset

The remaining chapters in this section will teach you to recognize the aspects of internal energy that are at work in each of your team members. In Section 3 you will learn a process for leveraging that energy to lead change.

4

Style

N ow that you are familiar with the concept of internal energy, you are ready to learn more about its three components.

HOW we do what we do
(Hands)

The first component of internal energy is our personal **Style**. Style is the term we use to describe the cluster of behaviors that each of us uses in our work lives. Style is often described as "how" we do what we do. Because it is possible to observe another person's style, we can also think of style as relating to the hands element of the head/heart/hands model.

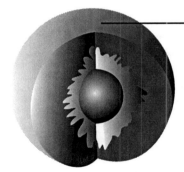
Style

As we discussed in Chapter 3, our style is on the surface—it's the first thing people see when they interact with us.

Since as early as 444 BC, philosophers and observers of human nature have noticed that:

- Individuals tend to behave fairly consistently over time.

- People's behaviors tend to fall into four clusters or categories.

In the late 1930s, Dr. William Moulton Marston observed that people generally behaved in one of four ways:

1. Some people were forceful, direct, and results-oriented.

2. Some people were optimistic, fun, and talkative.

3. Some people were steady, patient, and relaxed.

4. Some people were precise, accurate, and detail-oriented.

Researchers building on Marsten's work later developed a model now known as the DISC to explain and describe these four main styles of behavior. While the names of each category may differ according to each researcher, all use DISC as the easy-to-remember acronym.

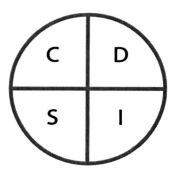

Marston's model is so robust and intuitive that you can begin to identify your own style and that of others after a quick introduction.*

Why DISC?

In our years in private practice, we've had the opportunity to sample many different behavioral instruments for use in personal development, leadership development, team development, etc. It became important for us to

---

* For a more formal and valid assessment of your own style, you might want to take the DISC assessment.

use an instrument that was easy to understand and one that was tied to business applications. It is also important for us to use an instrument that is supported by credible external validations and one that is continually updated based on the findings of these validation studies.

In our opinion, the DISC instrument, as developed in the late 1930s by Dr. William Moulton Marston, best fits these criteria. Marston's work was updated by Walter Clark in the 1950s, and later by Bill Bonnstetter beginning in the 1970s. Bonnstetter's research and applications continue today.[13] For this reason we use his instruments in our practice.

Over the past five years, DISC has increasingly become the behavior instrument of choice for organizations around the world, especially as it applies to team development, improved communication, and business development. DISC offers an observable, universal, gender-and-culture-neutral language that is easy to learn and apply across a wide array of business applications. It measures behaviors and emotions. It does not measure intelligence, values, or motivation; skills and experiences; or education and training.

Style Basics

In the following pages, you will learn the basics of style and the DISC model. Successive sections will explore deeper aspects of style and the ways in which style is a key element of understanding and unleashing the energy inherent in each person you work with.

Let's begin with a quick experiment. In the chart on the following page you will read about four styles that may or may not describe you. After reading the description, circle one word next to it to indicate whether you always, often, sometimes, almost never, or never fit the description.

Of course, you may use all of the behaviors once in a while depending on the situation. For now, however, please focus on how you act on a typical day in a normal situation.

I tend to be Forceful, Ambitious, Decisive, Challenging, Direct, and Independent	Always	Often	Sometimes	Almost Never	Never
I tend to be Expressive, Enthusiastic, Talkative, Demonstrative, Friendly, and Stimulating	Always	Often	Sometimes	Almost Never	Never
I tend to be Systematic, Methodological, Reliable, Relaxed, and Modest	Always	Often	Sometimes	Almost Never	Never
I tend to be Analytical, Contemplative, Conservative, Exacting, Careful, and Deliberate	Always	Often	Sometimes	Almost Never	Never

While your circling is a very unofficial assessment, you are starting to identify your primary work style(s).* Let's look at what that means.

If you always or often tend to be...	You may have a...
Forceful, Ambitious, Decisive, Challenging, Direct, and Independent	Driving Style
Expressive, Enthusiastic, Friendly, Demonstrative, Talkative, and Stimulating	Influencing Style
Systematic, Methodological, Reliable, Relaxed, and Modest	Steady Style
Analytical, Contemplative, Conservative, Exacting, Careful, and Deliberate	Careful Style

* This unscientific method depicts our conscious style—how we believe we need be in order to succeed or survive in our current roles. However, our more powerful subconscious styles can only be detected by using a more scientific assessment like the one used in our practice. For more information, please go to www.changeatthecore.com.

The developers of the DISC found that people normally had characteristics of two or three of these styles, but generally one behavior seemed to be the strongest—one that "popped" or stood out above all the rest. This is commonly referred to as their predominant style. Was there one description that "always" fits you? If so, that may be your predominant style.

Style Combinations

Some people's predominant style is actually a combination of two styles. For example, it is possible to have a Driving/Influencing Style (D/I) or a Driving/Steady (D/S) Style. As you may have guessed, a person with the D/I Style and a person with the D/S style have a great deal in common, yet they will still behave differently. Their Driving Style will be tempered by their secondary styles.

Do you have one preferred style? Or is your predominant style a combination? To find out, read more about each style on the following pages. As you read, consider your own style and begin to form some educated guesses about the styles of your team members and colleagues.

The Driving Style

18% of the general U.S. population[14]

- Fast-paced decision makers

- Competitive—like to win, dominate, and look for advantages

- Strong personality—impatient, direct, edgy

- Like to "control" the situation

- Focus on tasks and on achieving their personal agenda

Famous Examples

- Michael Jordan

- Barbara Walters

- Donald Trump

- Hilary Clinton

People You Know Who Best Match This Style

-
-
-

The Influential Style

29% of the general U.S. population

- High degree of people contact
- Optimistic, enthusiastic, passionate
- Talkers—friendly, likeable
- Like to "influence" the situation
- Focus on relationships and interactions with others

Famous Examples

- Oprah Winfrey
- President Bill Clinton
- Rosie O'Donnell
- Jamie Fox

People You Know Who Best Match This Style

-
-
-

The Steady Style

45% of the general U.S. population

- Organization-focused

- Patient, easy-going, reserved—never too high, never too low

- Planners—have a plan and work the plan to completion

- Like to trust people, products, and services

- Focus on processes, plans, and systems integration

Famous Examples

- Mr. Rogers

- Mother Theresa

- President Barak Obama

- Vijay Singh

People You Know Who Best Match This Style

-
-
-

The Careful Style

8% of the general U.S. population

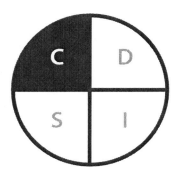

- Controllers
- Conservative, skeptical, suspicious
- Deliberate, logical thinkers with lots of questions
- Like facts, figures, analysis
- Focus on precision and minimizing risks or errors

Famous Examples

- Diane Sawyer
- Akan Greenspan
- Jack Nicklaus
- The Spock character from Star Trek

People You Know Who Best Match This Style

-
-
-

A Deeper Look at Styles

Now that you understand the fundamentals of style and the DISC model, let's turn our attention to a more advanced level of understanding.

As you read the previous section, you identified which style or styles are most comfortable for you. You may have made some educated guesses about the personal styles of people in your professional and personal life as well. This is a great start. Now let's take a deeper look.

While one or more styles may dominate our actions, each one of us actually demonstrates behaviors in all four dimensions. The Driving dimension is an indication of how you respond to problems and challenges. The Influence dimension is about how you deal with others. The Steady dimension gauges how you prefer to pace yourself and your work. The Careful dimension is about how you respond to rules and procedures.

D =	Your Style in Dealing with Problems
I =	Your Style in Dealing with People
S =	Your Style in Dealing with Pace
C =	Your Style in Dealing with Procedures

Consider yourself for a moment. Are you decisive in solving problems? If so, you probably "show" the Driving style. If you enjoy dealing with people, it's likely that you use a lot of Influencing behaviors, and so on.

In explaining the fact that all four dimensions are present in each of us, we like to refer to whether we "dial up" or "dial down" our behavior in each area.

The Driving Dimension—How We Handle Problems

People whose "D" dimension is dialed up are bold and aggressive in gaining results.

- They are decisive and action-oriented by nature.

- They are competitive and like to be in charge.

People whose "D" dimension is dialed down are more thoughtful about decision making.

- They want to consider all alternatives.

- They are more collaborative than competitive and like to make rational decisions for long-term gain.

These two groups often dispute the time it takes to make decisions. The Dialed-Up D's want to move quickly and the Dialed-Down D's want to make sure they get it right the first time.

> Charlie is a Dialed-Up D who is leading a new market entry project. Maureen, one of his teammates, is a Dialed-Down D.
>
> Charlie was anxious to get work started. He recommended that Maureen call around to a few people to briefly discuss their approach to new market entry, and then use what they learn to plan and implement their approach. Maureen pushed back on Charlie. She wanted to do her due diligence by researching the best practices in or order to fully understanding all of the ins and outs of new market entry. Then, and only then, would she feel comfortable designing an initial approach that could be vetted with others.
>
> By talking openly about their styles, Charlie and Maureen were able to agree on a middle ground to achieve their objective.

The Influencing Dimension—How We Handle People

People whose "I" dimension is dialed up are strongly networked both within and outside the organization.

- They are people-focused.

- They tend to be optimistic in good times and in bad.

- They really like to meet new people.

People whose "I" dimension is dialed down are much more analytical in nature than their counterparts.

- They are task-focused.

- They tend to be pessimistic in good times and in bad.

- They tend to meet fewer new people, but develop deep relationships with those they trust.

These two groups often dispute the amount of facts and due diligence required to move forward. Dialed-Up I's are more open to accepting people into their network. Dialed-Down I's would rather check all the facts and move more cautiously when dealing with people. They have a tighter circle of trust that can be hard to breach.

Kim was a Dialed-Up I in charge of leading a recruiting effort for experienced, technical managers. Joe was a Dialed-Down I who had been assigned to assist the recruiting team.

Kim was very excited about finding and hiring the perfect technical mangers for their area of specialization. Joe was much more skeptical. He found that the past candidates he had interviewed often talked a good game, but lacked the experiences, skills, or knowledge that were required in their company.

Kim and Joe leveraged each other's strengths by sharing the leadership role on this project. Kim was responsible for finding the candidates and convincing them to consider her company as a potential employer. Kim's ability to immediately connect with people and to get them to see the opportunities at her firm were astonishing. Meanwhile, Joe led the second interview team. He was sure to test each candidate's technical skills and to probe their experience. Both weighed in equally on the selection committee. As a result, the company was able to attract and select candidates who were truly the best fit for the job.

The Steady Dimension—How We Handle Pace

People whose "S" is dialed up must see things through to completion.

- They work at a steady, consistent pace with a focus on one task at a time.

- Being accommodating, adaptable, persistent and non-confrontational, they need time to mentally and emotionally adjust to change before jumping on board.

People whose "S" is dialed down are prototypical multitaskers who get bored easily with routine.

- They are great at brainstorming and starting initiatives.

- They like to hand their longer term work off to others for completion.

These two groups often dispute the path to success. Dialed-Up S's tend to have a plan and work their plan. Dialed-Down S's prefer to proactively try new things. They let the situation unfold and then act as needed.

Margaret, a Dialed-Up S, participated in a brainstorming session on how to improve the quality of her unit's services. Jake, a Dialed-Down S, participated in the same session.

As the meeting began, Jake's mind was racing and his mouth was running even faster. He spewed out one idea after another and was sure to show all the benefits associated with each of them. He dominated the conversation and left the room feeling quite pleased with himself and his efforts in moving the initiative forward.

Margaret sat in the meeting and was noticeably quiet. Even though she thought that most of Jake's ideas wouldn't hold water, she failed to express her opinion in the moment. She simply needed some time to absorb all the information presented, then to think about the alternatives and their pros and cons. The following day, Margaret approached the team with ideas on how to proceed. Jake immediately jumped up and started to round out her ideas. Together they came up with a better solution than either of them could have developed independently. The team leveraged both of these key resources to develop a workable, productive, and effective quality improvement plan.

The Careful Dimension—How We Handle Procedures

People whose "C" is dialed up are precise, accurate, and quality-oriented.

- They pay a great deal of attention to detail—they would rather deal with the trees than the forest. In fact, they would like to deal with a specific tree in the forest.

- They need time to ask questions so that they can be sure to understand the exact situation and what's needed.

People whose "C" is dialed down dislike being held to tight rules, roles, and procedures unless they define them for themselves.

- They would rather deal at a high level and assign or delegate the detail checking to others—they prefer to deal with the forest than the trees.

- They can feel bogged down and drained when dealing with details.

These two groups often dispute the amount of control required in any given situation. Dialed-Up C's tend to be perfectionists. Dialed-Down C's prefer to deal with the overviews and spend little time on controlling every detail.

Paul, a Dialed-Up C, was in charge of Information Services (IS) for a large corporation. Paul's team was tasked with creating proprietary software and installing the hardware to run it.

Paul's colleague, Chris—a Dialed-Down C—was in charge of marketing and communications. Chris constantly came up with ideas for new internal communication tools that Paul's team then had to create and implement. Paul thought many of Chris's ideas were "hare-brained" and poorly thought-out. Chris always underestimated the time and costs the projects would require. Paul attempted to get Chris to think things through more carefully, but both left their conversations feeling frustrated with the other.

After Paul and Chris learned the DISC model and shared their natural styles, they understood why their interactions had been so frustrating. They learned to partner with each other—relying on Chris to continue developing ideas and counting on Paul to figure out which plans were feasible.

Benefits of Understanding Styles

There are many benefits to understanding styles:

- Understanding styles helps to prevent and reduce conflict.

- Adapting your style to match the style of a colleague or client dramatically increases the effectiveness of communications between you.

- The most effective way to gain the cooperation and commitment of others is to interact with them in their preferred style.

Styles Are Adaptable

To some extent our style is hard-wired. We use a certain style so much over our lifetime that it becomes almost habit. The good news is that, when necessary, we can adapt our style.

Awareness Helps Us Adapt

We were working with a software development company's executive team on a weekend retreat. The CEO greeted us outside of the room. He said he needed some coaching help because immediately after the weekend he intended to fire Pat, the chief technical officer of the firm. He said that of anyone in the company, Pat caused the most stress within and throughout the organization. He said that this could no longer be tolerated.

Later that morning, we introduced the DISC model and gave the team members their personal assessment results. We then asked each executive to "stand and declare" their preferred style(s). As we got halfway around the room, Pat stood to address the group. He said, "Oh my goodness. I just realized that you are all very different than me. I've been approaching you in my style, not in yours. You must think I'm a buffoon!*" As heads nodded, Pat went on to say, "From this point on, I'll try to recognize your style and appreciate our differences. I can't guarantee that I'll always do this perfectly. If I don't, please call me on it."

Needless to say the other members of the executive team were somewhat skeptical. Still, the CEO delayed his discussion with Pat. Two weeks later he called us to report that other employees throughout the organization were asking, "Who did the lobotomy on Pat?" There was no lobotomy—only a clearer understanding of behavior style.

Two years later we attended a gala event to celebrate a milestone anniversary for the firm. At the end of the evening, the CEO announced the winner of the company's Most Valuable Employee award. Pat was greeted at the podium by a rousing round of applause.

While we can learn to adapt our styles, it is important to remember that our style is a source of energy for us. When we get to behave in alignment with our predominant style, we feel energized and excited about our work. Acting "out of style" can be done, but it is often draining and de-energizing. As you will learn in later chapters, understanding and leveraging the other two elements of internal energy (passion and mindset) are key to our ability to adapt and to help others adapt as needed.

The "I Can Do That If…" Technique

As we go through our day, our intention is to do the best job possible with what we have available to us. Yet even with the best of intentions, things may not go smoothly. While there could be many reasons for this, the one reason that applies directly to one's style is that people sometimes are asked to do things in a way that is totally contrary to their best

---

* In reality, Pat didn't use the word buffoon. He actually used a more colorful word.

personal method of operation. Being asked to continually stretch beyond our personal styles causes a great deal of anxiety and undue stress.

For example, some styles are more assertive than their opposite types. People who exhibit these styles may push their staff or teammates to make decisions much more quickly than their styles prefer. Those who don't have enough time to study the facts, alternatives and options before they make their decisions may begin to feel anxiety and stress. If this pattern continues, it can lead to burnout.

There is a technique we teach that allows one to push back against such work demands in order to set one's self up for success. We call it the "I Can Do That If…" technique. Generally we've found that if someone asks us to do something for him or her, they don't want to hear the word "can't." All they want to know is what we "can" do and not what we "can't" do for them. To illustrate this point:

I. Dialed-Up D's and I's and Dialed-Down S's and C's want things done right now.

II. Dialed-Down D's and I's and Dialed-Up S's and C's want things done absolutely right.

If you are in group II and find yourself feeling pressured by a person from group I to get it done "right now," try saying "I Can Do That If…"

- You give me a few minutes to think about it.

- You make this my top priority.

- I can have until tomorrow to complete my research.

- You stop standing over me and give me some time to review the facts.

Reactions to Change

As you saw in each example on the previous pages, understanding style differences can help you connect, communicate, and collaborate more effectively with others.

We've also discovered that an understanding of styles can be a powerful advantage in communicating change and building a base of support. To understand this, it is helpful to understand how people with each style react to change.

- People with the **Driving Style** thrive on shaking things up. Since is it almost impossible for a Dialed-Up D *not* to change things, it is often the D's who initiate change.

- Those who prefer the **Influencing Style** are quick to support change when their opinions are sought. They relish opportunities to act as catalysts and to engage others.

- People who prefer a **Steady Style** are much less likely to commit to a change at the outset. As a whole, they prefer incremental change. When you propose a change, these folks will show little or no reaction at first. They are watching other people's reactions and weighing the proposed solution.

- Finally, people who gravitate toward the **Careful Style** are skeptical. They will want to see compelling reasons (data) for the change and they will be slow to support change unless they agree that there is a significant problem and a well-thought-out solution. Alternatively, if a system, process, or procedure fails to work effectively, people with a Careful Style will push for change because they can't live with imprecision.

Implications for Communicating Change

In a common scenario, a leader will announce a change and hope everyone in the organization will quickly support the effort. What usually happens instead is that the announcement is followed by silence.

A few Drivers (18 percent of the general population) may say, "We should do it" and start to assign people to tasks. When the Influencers (29 percent) see that the drivers are serious, they may start talking about how to get things moving. At this point, only 47 percent of the group has made up their minds to support the change.

Now the people who prefer a Careful Style (8 percent) will jump in and start to poke holes into the plans. Their talent for logical thinking and need for precision translates into doubt and skepticism.

Most leaders naturally respond by attempting to answer every question the C's raise at this point. Often they find themselves going down a rabbit hole as deeper issues are uncovered. The part of the team who prefers the Steady Style (45 percent) quietly observe as they watch the interaction. When the D's and I's don't have the answers to all of the C's questions, the S's conclude that the change is too risky and balk at moving forward.

An Alternative—Tipping Point Communication

Instead of falling into the trap described above, leaders can take a page from Malcolm Gladwell, author of *The Tipping Point*. Gladwell's book focuses on how great ideas are propelled forward when key people (connectors) show their support and influence enough other people to "tip" public opinion.[15]

In the example we saw above, the change effort stalled out due to a lack of support. What would have happened if the leader could have used the tipping point technique? Instead of taking time out to address all of the C's questions, the leader could have focused on asking the Influencers to connect and communicate with the Steady Style team members. With the D's, I's, and S's in agreement, the numbers would tip far in favor of the initiative. This doesn't mean you should not address the C's concerns. You need this group's attention to detail to find the holes in the plan and mitigate them. You just don't want to allow this group's skepticism to stall an effort before it begins!

Chapter Highlights

In today's world of work, the most critical resource is time. Managers often strive to add resources or reengineer processes or systems to make them more efficient. Until now, actions like these were the only means available to provide more time and capacity into the workday. Now we know that assigning people to work that they naturally do well increases effectiveness and reduces the time and mental errors that occur when one is assigned to a task that does not fit his/her individual style.

As a change leader, you can use your understanding of styles to:

- Connect with people on the dimension that most excites and energizes them.

- Assign people responsibilities and tasks that leverage their personal energy and style.

You'll learn more about leveraging styles in Section 3.

Just for Fun

John Kotter's book, *Our Iceberg Is Melting*, features four penguins that make up the leadership team for a colony in crisis.[16] When we read the book, it was immediately apparent that the four penguin leaders represent the four DISC styles. Can you match the character to its style? The answers can be found in Appendix A.

Alice—the tough, practical penguin who had a reputation for getting things done fast.

Style: _____

Louis—the calm and reflective head penguin who could always read the energy of the group.

Style: _____

Jordan—the logical penguin who often asked intellectual questions and was known as "The Professor."

Style: _____

Buddy—the penguin that did away with PowerPoint and told a compelling story.

Style: _____

5

Passion

The second component of internal energy is our Passion. *Passion* is the term we use to describe what moves and motivates us to take action.

Because our passion reflects our inner feelings and motivations, we can relate passion to the heart aspect of the head/heart/hands model.

Passion: WHY we do what we do (Heart)

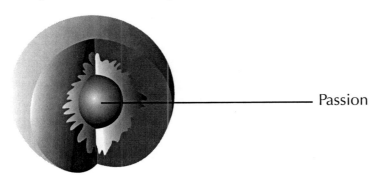 —————— Passion

As this diagram illustrates, our passion is at the very center of our core. Our passion is what motivates us.

Researchers have identified six culture-neutral, gender-neutral core motivators.

- Passion for Knowledge
- Passion for Results
- Passion for Creativity
- Passion for People

- Passion for Leading

- Passion for Tradition

Each of these six passions is present in all of us to differing extents. The real power lies in being able to identify each person's top one or two passions. This will enable us to understand WHY a person will move toward one thing (an event, a project, a work assignment, a group or team, etc.) and away from another.

Assessing Passions

Research in the area of measuring a person's motivation and values dates back to the work of the German psychologist, teacher, and philosopher Eduard Spranger and his 1928 publication, "Types of Men." Spranger proposed that there are six basic types of attitudes. While all six attitudes may be present in each of us, our top two really move us to action. His belief was that these attitudes were predetermined, so people should learn to understand them and be who they are.[17] Bill Bonnstetter further defined Spranger's seminal work over the years. Bonnstetter developed the first sophisticated assessment tool based on the six attitudes of Spranger in 1990. In later years, he refined the instrument for use in business settings and created the Workplace Motivators (WPM) assessment.[18] We now use the WPM to assess one's passion, motivations, or values in the workplace.

Understanding our own passions, and those of others, is therefore helpful in leading change, selecting team members, making assignments, and communicating with others.

Read more about each passion on the following pages—first to understand your own personal passions and then to form some educated guesses about the passions of your team members and colleagues.

Passion for Knowledge

People with a passion for knowledge have a distinct intellectual curiosity. They need to understand how things work and why they work the way they do. These people are generally considered by others to be intellectual. They are eager learners interested in new methods and how they can be applied to existing situations. As continuous lifelong learners, they are objective and nonjudgmental. They like to use their knowledge to be the expert in their chosen field.

Key Words and Phrases

Learn, Understand, Curious, Know, Deeper Meaning, Smart, Wise, Intelligent, Analyze, etc.

People You Know Who Fit this Description

-
-
-

Passion for Results

Those with a passion for results value personal and organizational accomplishments. They are naturally drawn to work that allows them to have a bottom-line impact. These folks are pragmatic, practical, and adept at doing just what is necessary to achieve the business result. They are resourceful at optimizing the physical, financial, and human resources available to them. They like to be rewarded through a combination of financial means, recognition, career opportunities and other areas of perceived value in exchange for their investment of time, energy, and resources to the enterprise.

Key Words and Phrases

Practical, Productive, Return on Investment (ROI), Useful, Earn, Invest, Achieve, Bottom Line, etc.

People You Know Who Fit this Description

-
-
-

Passion for Creativity

People with a passion for creativity have a personal value for self-expression. They may be creative in the artistic sense with a keen interest in the fine arts (music, dance, art) or in some other creative activity (photography, crafts, writing, etc.). In the work environment, these people can be very creative, imaginative, and innovative in developing and portraying new products and services. They also strive to maintain harmony in their work environment and in their work-life balance. These folks do need some solitary time for reflection and re-balancing their work lives.

Key Words and Phrases

Create, Harmony, Balance, Appreciate, Work/Life Balance, Time to Reenergize, etc.

People You Know Who Fit this Description

-
-
-

Passion for People

People with a passion for people are altruistic. They value opportunities to serve others and to contribute to the higher good of their groups, teams, families, or organizations. These folks are often called humanitarians. They have a strong drive to help others learn and grow. At work, these people freely volunteer to help others. They make good teachers, coaches, and mentors. They are strong team players and will often put others before themselves. They may also find themselves attracted to not-for-profit organizations and/or caregiver roles.

Key Words and Phrases

Help You, Serve, Contribute, Teach, Coach, Humanity, Connect, Volunteer, People, etc.

People You Know Who Fit this Description

-
-
-

Passion for Leading

People with a passion for leading have a strong drive to express their personal power. They like to be seen as unique and distinctive and as the "go to" person in times of crisis. As leaders of the pack, they work very hard to be #1. They are assertive, determined, adaptable, and spontaneous in work that gives them a sense of "standing" and respect in the eyes of others. They are quick to recover from adversity. They like to be positioned in a niche where they can excel and stand out in the marketplace. When the going gets tough, these people naturally rise to the occasion.

Key Words and Phrases

Lead, Be #1, The Best, Energetic, Distinctive, Excel, Power, Succeed, etc.

People You Know Who Fit this Description

-
-
-

Passion for Tradition

People with a passion for tradition uphold values, rules, and regulations. They are the standard bearers of traditional organizations and can be seen as the guardians of the corporate culture. They are structured, orderly, and precise in their approaches to their work and to their lives. They work extremely well with others who share their high standards and values. They will often sacrifice themselves for a cause.

Key Words and Phrases

Standards, Discipline, Protocol, Chain of Command, Stability, Beliefs, Routines, Sacrifice, etc.

People You Know Who Fit this Description

-
-
-

We Aren't Always Aware of Our Own Passions!

Over the years, we have learned that it is often difficult to discern our passions from our styles. This may be because our style is observable on the surface, while passion is more internal and not readily observable without questions, considerations, and probing.

Here's an example:

We were using the Workplace Motivators assessment as part of coaching the CEO of a medium-sized business. When this person saw that in her hierarchy, her number one motivator was Passion for People and her number five motivator was Passion for Creativity, she railed against the results. She said, "This simply cannot be accurate. When I was in high school, I entered a number of community art contests and I always won the blue ribbons. That's Creativity, not People." When we asked her, "WHY did you enter the art contests?" she replied, "All my friends and family would come to support me, and I got to meet a lot of new people whom I am still friends with today. Not only that, but when I would win one of these contests, I would donate both my picture and the blue ribbon to the charity sponsoring the event. They would use these to gain supplemental funding for their events and charities in silent auctions held later that evening."

As we can see, the CEO's reason for entering the art contests was fueled by her Passion for People. Her art was simply one vehicle for achieving her personal passion.

Passion and Influence

Because our passions are largely subconscious and because our passions drive our choices and behaviors, they represent the most powerful element of internal energy. Marketers and salespeople have known for decades that success in influencing consumers comes down to being able to plug into their passions.

While you aren't "selling" per se, a great deal of your success as a change leader will depend on your ability to influence and engage other people. Passions are a powerful tool for doing so.

Just for Fun

There are several popular product and service advertisements we hear and see each and every day. Can you guess the passions of the target audiences for the following taglines? The answers can be found in Appendix A.

U.S. Marines—The Few, The Proud, The Marines

Lexus—Pursuit Of Perfection

Campbell's Soup—M'm. M'm. Good

Harvard University—Learning Together

General Electric—We Bring Good Things to Life

Oakland Raiders (Al Davis)—Just Win Baby

Leveraging Passions to Lead Change

As a change leader, you can use your understanding of passions to:

- Identify people's priorities and motivations

- Recognize what may be behind people's responses to change

- Talk about a change initiative in way that will motivate people to want to participate

Imagine for a moment that you are able to identify each of your teammates' highest areas of passion or motivation. With this knowledge you could begin to assign people to change initiatives based on where their passion lies. You could also use this insight to shape internal communications to quickly get people committed to the system, process, procedure, and people changes that accompany every major change initiative.

The paragraphs below describe how people with each passion respond to change initiatives.

Passion for Knowledge

These people can play a key role in research, benchmarking, analysis of systems, and development projects where a strong knowledge base is required. They are also very good at finding the best processes, procedures, and systems from two merged companies to be integrated into the new enterprise.

Passion for Results

These people are strong at finding ways to gain a competitive advantage. They are especially adept at identifying value propositions for new products and services that may result from a change.

Passion for Creativity

These people are strong at quickly bringing order to chaos. Since they need harmony in their lives, they will work to creatively get the organization through the change and back to the steady state as soon as possible.

Passion for People

These people are strong at focusing on the people impact of the change. They will be sure that no one gets left behind.

Passion for Leading

These people are strong at leading the change effort. They will confidently communicate the vision, mission, and values of the new organization both internally and externally.

Passion for Tradition

These people will initially resist a change effort if it negatively impacts their values and standards. However, once committed, these folks will work long and hard to establish and maintain performance standards and corporate values across the enterprise.

The "I Wish I Knew..." Technique

Passion and resistance are often closely connected. If people feel that a change violates or jeopardizes what matters most to them, they will respond with resistance. If not addressed head-on, resistance can derail our change initiatives. One of the most effective ways we know of to proactively deal with resistance is to use the "I wish I knew..." (IWIK) technique early in the change communication process. Here's how it works.

After announcing a change initiative and explaining all the reasons for moving in this new direction, ask your audience: (1) "What do you LIKE about this change?" This elicits the audience's view on the benefits of the change. Do not move forward until you have at least a few benefits, no matter how draconian the change might seem. Don't worry. In a broad audience, someone will see some benefits to the new approach. (2) Ask the audience, "What questions or concerns do you have about this change? You can say anything you'd like as long as you begin your statement with the words, *'I wish I knew...'* ".

The IWIK technique allows the audience members to express their points of view—to get their emotional concerns off their chests and out into the open where they can be dealt with more rationally. Using the words, "I wish I knew..." transforms the emotion or "gripe" into a problem statement. As a change leader, it gives you a heads up on the underlying concerns within the organization and a pathway for moving forward. If you can address the concerns, the change initiative will move faster and smoother.

If you are on the receiving end of a change, the IWIK statement gives you an elegant way of expressing your concern without it sounding overly critical or judgmental. As such, it protects both the messenger and receiver.

Chapter Highlights

Once we understand someone's passion hierarchy, we are able to explain their internal decision-making criteria. Passions capture what we value. When we have to make a choice, our passions dictate our choices, even when we aren't consciously aware of it.

6

Mindset

The second component of internal energy is our personal *Mindset*. Mindset is the term we use to describe a person's mental framework—what one thinks and feels is important in performing one's job. Mindset can also be thought of as what we focus on.

Mindset:

WHAT we focus on (Head)

Because our mindset reflects the thoughts that are top-of-mind when working in a business situation, we can relate mindset to the *head* aspect of the head/heart/hands model.

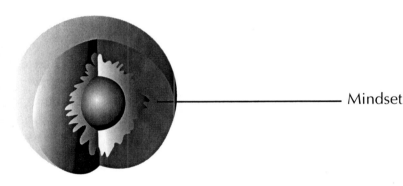

— Mindset

As this diagram illustrates, our mindset acts as sort of a filter between our passion and our style. Our mindset determines where our energy is focused. When dealing with the world around us, there are three primary areas of focus that compete for our attention. They are:

- People—A focus on the people around us, our customers, colleagues, and suppliers, etc.

- Processes—A focus on the procedures, processes, and routines that we employ to do our work.

- Systems—A focus on the broader vision of our organization, the mission, values, approaches, rules of play, etc., and how each of these elements are aligned and connected.

Naturally, all three mindsets are crucial. Depending on the situation, we may need to change our mindset to focus more on one area versus another.

The Connection between Mindset and Behaviors

Research has found that our styles (Driving, Influencing, Steady, or Careful) are somewhat hard-wired. Each day we act in accordance with the style we are saddled with. We may be able to dial up or dial down a behavior in a specific situation, but it is awfully hard for most of us to change who we are. Nor should we! Each of our styles contributes to the diversity and health of our work environment.

At the same time, there are situations where relying only on our personal style can create problems and impede our performance. For example, a manager who prefers the Influencing Style may be great at inspiring people, but may completely overlook the tools, systems, and processes that people need to do their jobs. A person who excelled as a technical expert because of his Careful Style may struggle when promoted to a leadership role that requires him to be able to connect with people.

Fortunately, there is a work-around for one's style—one's mindset. What you focus on or pay attention to can affect the end result. When we consciously shift our mindset or mental framework, we can train ourselves to pay attention to the things we may miss when operating out of our personal style. For an example of shifting mindsets, check out the story on the following page.

The key thing to remember about mindsets is that by being deliberate and intentional in what you ask your team to focus on, you can help people break out of their typical habits and natural reactions.

Managing Mike's Mindset

Mike and Elaine worked for a large Fortune 20 company. In addition to their day jobs, both were often tapped to work on special initiatives. On one such assignment, they were part of a team responsible for the complete restructuring of a major international division of their company. Their efforts were so successful that Elaine was chosen to be the CFO of the new organization. She quickly picked Mike to lead the financial services function within her portfolio.

Almost immediately, the once-collegial relationship between Mike and Elaine turned confrontational. Each seemed to be getting in the other's way and on the other's nerves. Disagreements on almost every approach to implementing the new organization became competitive jousting matches. After about one month, Mike couldn't take the stress any longer. He reached for the phone and called Elaine. When she answered, she said, "This is incredible. I was just about to call you. Can you come see me for a few minutes?"

When they met, Elaine began, "Mike, I promoted you two levels because I knew you were exactly the right person for this job. Here's the thing: There are some things you did in your past job that were very effective. Some of those things you need to keep in the current job. Others, you'll have to leave behind because they won't serve you in your current position. For example, your intense focus on getting results is admirable. However, in this position a more important focus for you is long-range and conceptual thinking. I need you to lead your organization to where it's never been before."

This brief conversation hit Mike like a ton of bricks. He knew exactly what Elaine was talking about. He also knew that she was right. Mike had always had an Influencing/Driving Style. In team meetings he was the optimist encouraging others to stay with the task at hand until they cracked the code on the problem. At times, he was too quick to take the initial recommendations and run with them in his zeal to get things done. In fact, he prided himself in being a "doer." Throughout his career he had always been rewarded for his sense of urgency and responsiveness in day-to-day operations and for his leadership abilities.

Their conversation helped Mike realize that while his natural style had served him well in the past, it was not the style needed now. In his new position, he needed to be focused on the long-term strategic direction of the function. His new role required him to be less of doer and more of a thinker. Mike needed to transition to a Systems Mindset and adapt his style to be more Careful and Steady.

The "Because" Technique

Many years ago, Xerox hired a professional linguistics group to study the effect words had on convincing people to openly consider their products versus the competition's. In the study, an employee was asked to barge into a line of people waiting to make copies and say something like, "I need to make a copy of this now." The researchers then tested the people in line to see how many of them were upset by the disruption. 68 percent reported being annoyed and upset about someone attempting to cut into the line.

Sometime later, the same employee was again asked to barge into the copy line, but this time she was to say, "I need to make a copy of this now BECAUSE my boss needs me to make him a copy." The people in the line were again surveyed to see if they minded the disruption. Researchers found that 98 percent of the people surveyed didn't actually mind the disruption when the employee used the word "because."

After another brief break, the employee was asked to barge into the line a third time. This time she was instructed to say, "I need to make a copy of this now BECAUSE I need to make a copy of this now." This time the surveys found that 97 percent of the people surveyed didn't actually mind the disruption when the employee used the word "because," even though the sentence that was used didn't make much sense to the listener.

As a change leader, to change someone's mindset, you need to tell your audience why the change is (1) important to the organization; and (2) important to you personally. As you communicate these key messages, be sure to use the word "because." In this way, you'll give people a reason to change their mindset.

Leading Change through Mindset

In addition to recognizing the power of individual mindsets, you can use your understanding of mindsets to help you as you form change teams. As you may have guessed, every change team needs to include a subset of people who deliberately focus on the people, process, and systems aspects of an initiative in order for change to be successful.

As the table below illustrates, different mindsets result in different actions by the change team. These actions in turn lead to differing results.

People with this Mindset	Tend to create...	Which tends to result in...
People	Events designed to engage and communicate with employees at all levels	Employees feeling valued Strong business and social relationships
Processes	Detailed project plans Clear roles and responsibilities	Procedures and processes' being in sync People having the tools to do their jobs
Systems	Alignment between functions Integrated communication and development plans	People understanding where the organization is headed People feeling positively about belonging to the organization

Leading Change through All Three Mindsets

The internal computing function of a major Internet service provider was in the midst of reorganizing its operations around a balanced scorecard-management system. Early in the process, its leadership team put together its vision, mission, values, and key pathways to success in the format of a high-level strategy map. The change leaders decided to vet their strategic approach with both the general population of employees and internal customers in a series of workshops.

In the workshops, the leaders presented an overview of their plans and the details on how new processes would work. Employees were asked to provide their feedback on the viability of the approach. They were asked:

- What do you like about the approach?

- What could be better?

- What's missing and needs to be included for this to make a difference?

Thanks to the feedback, the leadership team was able to make changes to both their strategic approach and the specific processes being proposed.

In this example, the leadership team effectively tapped into all three mindsets—people, process, and systems. The original project plans and requests for feedback were focused on **Processes.** By conducting the workshops, in addition to improving processes, the team members learned that they needed to increase their focus on **People**—both their own staff and their internal customers. They also had to take more of a **Systems** view of their work to ensure that their strategic direction was in sync with the broader organization.

Chapter Highlights

Change leaders recognize that for organizational transformation to succeed, all three mindsets (People, Processes, and Systems) must be taken into account. Fortunately, we can deliberately shift our own mindsets and those of others.

As you'll discover in Chapter 7, an understanding of mindsets, coupled with an understanding of styles and passions, is a powerful tool for any change leader.

SECTION THREE

Leading Change at the Core

"If everyone is moving forward together,
then success takes care of itself."
–Unknown

7

Leading Change at the Core

In Section 2, you learned about the three components of internal energy: style, passion, and mindset. In this section, you will learn the specific steps for leveraging that internal energy to lead change successfully.

Leading change is about getting wholehearted commitment—one person at a time.

Change Requires Commitment

In our view, leading change is about getting wholehearted commitment—one person at a time. We agree with Thomas Herrington and Patrick Malone, who write, "Wholehearted implies leaders have engaged their followers emotionally and intellectually—both in the heart and head. Wholehearted also implies that the follower decides whether or not to give his or her commitment."[19]

Or, as a famous leader once said,

> "You do not lead by hitting people over the head
> —that's assault, not leadership."
> ~ Dwight D. Eisenhower

So how do you gain wholehearted commitment?

Energy + Engagement =
Commitment

The Importance of Engagement

We like to think of internal energy as the secret ingredient of commitment. But, of course, energy alone is not enough to power change. In fact, you could say that energy is necessary, but not sufficient.

The second element of gaining wholehearted commitment is engagement. As experts from Duke Corporate Education wrote, "Companies frequently find themselves in the midst of a need to change direction, culture, partners, and/or positioning .... Execution, the ability to actually do it, and do it well, starts with engaged people, people who understand the strategy, believe it is meaningful to them and understand how they personally can contribute to its success."[20]

Leading Change at the Core

The Change at the Core process combines an understanding of energy with the skills of engagement. The four key steps to leading Change at the Core are:

1. Understand each person's internal energy.

2. Connect and communicate to promote openness to change.

3. Understand, appreciate, and address resistance.

4. Align and unleash each person's energy to power the change.

The Change at the Core Process

1. Understand each person's internal energy.

2. Connect and communicate to promote openness to change.

3. Understand, appreciate, and address resistance.

4. Align and unleash each person's energy to power the change.

Leveraging energy is something you do with people— not to them.

In the following chapters, you will learn tips, techniques, and suggestions for each of these steps. You will also have the opportunity to learn from the stories of other leaders who have used these skills and techniques.

Caveats and Cautions

Before we go into more detail, however, we want to address two philosophical points.

- Leveraging energy is something you do with people—not to them.

- To gain the commitment needed to lead change, you need to be able to let go of having all the answers.

Leveraging Energy Is Something You Do with People—Not to Them

We've seen Change at the Core in action enough to know what a powerful process it is. Unfortunately there are always a few people in any organization who think that this process will give them a "leg up over others." We want to be clear that leveraging energy is something you do in partnership with others. The idea is not to "psych out" other people or to trick them into accepting a change. We want you and your team to have the words to speak each other's language and the tools to talk openly in a way that energizes everyone involved.

Let Go of Having All the Answers

Here's a key to remember: To get people to commit to a change, you have to let go of having all of the answers.

Management guru Peter Block points out that many of us approach interactions with others as an opportunity to get them to go along with us. He states that this rather Machiavellian approach causes people to distrust us and resist our solutions. Instead, he advocates having conversations. Conversations are two-way dialogues—opportunities to explore, understand, and create meaning.[21]

You have to let go of having all of the answers.

Now, we know you are thinking, "What a minute! Doesn't that take a long time? What happens when I'm in a hurry and I need people to change now?" The reality comes back to compliance versus commitment. If we want others to own the solution, it needs to come from within them.

And remember, change is an iterative process. As you learn from your team members, you are moving closer to a shared vision of the future. And, as the destination becomes clearer, it becomes easier for people to take definitive action to get there. Isn't that what you want? For others in the company to be just as committed as you are? For others to take action without waiting for directives from you?

Letting Go

We recently worked with Charlie, the CEO of a growing technology company on the East coast. Charlie had spent several months working on a new operating model for his company. The new model would significantly grow revenue and attract venture capital. Charlie had worked with a well-known consulting company to identify his vision, develop supporting strategies, and create a visual model that represented how the company would operate in the future. As you might imagine, Charlie was proud of what he had developed and eager to get the people in his organization to execute his vision.

Charlie had nine direct reports who made up his executive team. Being a savvy leader, Charlie met individually with each of these leaders to share his vision. A week later, he called his team into a two-day off-site meeting. The goal of the meeting was to get "final" support for the model and then spend two days working out the details.

You can probably guess what happened . . . RESISTANCE. Instead of quickly supporting the model, the leaders hemmed and hawed. They looked at the floor. They looked at the ceiling. Finally someone spoke up and said it seemed to be missing something. Suddenly heads were nodding and others started to chime in.

At first we thought Charlie was going to explode!! His face turned seven shades of red and he balled his hands into fists. We really thought Charlie was going to start pounding the table and telling everyone to "just get on board."

To his credit, he didn't. We'd been coaching Charlie on how to let go of having all of the answers. We saw him take a deep breath. He monitored his tone and volume and he calmly said, "It looks as if this model isn't working for everyone. Could we go around the table and ask each person to share what components you do support?" After gathering the first round of input, Charlie then asked the team to share concerns using the "I wish I knew..." technique described in Chapter 5.

Ahh! It was all we could do not to break into applause!! Instead we quietly watched as the group engaged in a productive dialogue about the operating model. It took a day, but by dinner time, the group had jointly developed a model that they were all happy with, and more importantly, deeply committed to. At the time Charlie didn't know it, but he was demonstrating his own skill at leading Change at the Core.

Chapter Highlights

The Change at the Core process is a powerful tool for any change leader. Remember though, it is not a trick and it is not something you do to people. Effective change comes about when leaders and their teams communicate to close the change gap.

Now that you have seen the steps of the Change at the Core process, let's look at the specifics of how to implement them. The next four chapters are devoted to each of the four steps.

> "Change imposed is not change effected."
> ~ John Kotter, Harvard Professor

8

Understanding Each Person's Internal Energy

When implementing Change at the Core, Step 1 is to understand each of your people's internal energy.

In Section 2, you learned that each person on your team has a combination of elements at his/her core that make up his/her internal energy. These elements include:

Step 1 of the Change at the Core process is to understand each of your people's internal energy.

Style

- Driving Style

- Influencing Style

- Steady Style

- Careful Style

Passion

- Passion for Knowledge

- Passion for Results

- Passion for Creativity

- Passion for People

- Passion for Leading

- Passion for Tradition

Mindset

- People

- Processes

- Systems

Let's now take these elements and begin to apply them to your team. Even without an official assessment, you may have been able to form some guesses about the styles, passions, and mindsets of your people. Take a few minutes now to jot down your observations below. If you are not sure, or don't have enough data to come to a conclusion, just leave that section blank. This is simply a tool to help you begin to apply what you are learning.

Tool: Style Chart

D Dimension = How Your Team Members Deal with Problems

Style	Clues	Team Members
↑ **Dialed-Up D**	• They are bold and aggressive in gaining results. • They are decisive by nature and action-oriented. • They are competitive and like to be in charge.	
←→ **Middle D**		
Dialed-Down D ↓	• They are thoughtful about decision making. • They want to consider all alternatives. • They are more collaborative than competitive and like to make rational decisions for long-term gain.	

Style Chart, continued

I Dimension = How Your Team Members Deal with People

Style	Clues	Team Members
↑ **Dialed-Up I**	• They are strongly networked both within and outside the organization. • They are people-focused and optimistic in good times and in bad. • They really like to meet new people.	
←→ **Middle I**		
Dialed-Down I ↓	• They are much more analytical in nature than their counterparts. • They are task-focused and pessimistic in good times and in bad. • They tend to meet fewer new people, but develop deep relationships with those they trust.	

S Dimension = How Your Team Members Deal with Pace

*Style Chart,
continued*

Style	Clues	Team Members
↑ **Dialed-Up S**	• They must see things through to completion. • They work at a steady, consistent pace with a focus on one task at a time. • They need time to mentally and emotionally adjust to change before committing.	
←→ **Middle S**		
Dialed-Down S ↓	• They are prototypical multitaskers who get bored easily with routine. • They are great at brain-storming and starting initiatives. • They like to hand their longer-term work off to others for completion.	

Style Chart,
continued

C Dimension = How Your Team Members Deal with Procedures

Style	Clues	Team Members
↑ **Dialed-Up C**	• They are precise, accurate, and quality-oriented. • They pay a great deal of attention to detail. • They need time to ask questions so they can understand the exact situation and what's needed.	
←→ **Middle C**		
Dialed-Down C ↓	• They dislike being held to tight rules, roles, and procedures unless they define them for themselves. • They would rather deal at a high level and assign or delegate the details to others. • They can feel bogged down and drained when dealing with details.	

Tool: Passion Chart

Passion	Clues	Team Members
Knowledge	• They need to understand how why things work the way they do. • They are eager learners and are interested in applying new methods to existing situations. • They like to use their knowledge to be the expert in their chosen field.	
Results	• They are naturally drawn to work that allows them to have a bottom-line impact. • They are pragmatic and practical. • They like to be rewarded through a combination of financial means, public recognition, and career opportunities.	

Passion	Clues	Team Members
Creativity	• They have a personal value for self-expression. • They can be very creative, imaginative, and innovative in developing and portraying new products and services. • They strive to maintain harmony in their work environment.	
People	• They value opportunities to serve others and to contribute to the higher good of their groups, teams, families, or organizations. • They have a strong drive to help others learn and grow. • They are strong team players who will often put others before themselves.	

Passion	Clues	Team Members
Leading	• They like to be seen as unique and distinctive and the go-to person in times of crisis. • They work very hard to be #1. • They are assertive, determined, and adaptable.	
Tradition	• They uphold traditions, values, and regulations and are often the guardians of corporate culture. • They are structured, orderly, and precise in their approach to their work and to their lives. • They will often sacrifice themselves for a cause.	

Passion Chart, continued

Tool: Mindset Chart

Mindset	Clues	Team Members
People	• They place importance on diversity of thought, styles, and passions and want to build strong relationships with people they work with.	
Processes	• They are focused on the details of the computer systems, work processes, procedural steps, etc., needed to get the job done.	
Systems	• They look for alignment within and across functions/departments and processes.	

Once you have finished, take a look back at your charts. Do you have a lot of question marks? That's not unusual. It can be difficult to come to conclusions without having other means to validate or negate your impression. Having listed your own observations, it is now critical for you to confirm or revise your assumptions.

We strongly suggest that you talk with each of your team members about their internal energy. In particular, you might discover that people's passions and mindsets are different than what you initially thought. You may also want to consider asking each of your team members to take the assessments that measure styles, passions, and mindsets.

With or without the formal assessments, we believe that a general understanding of the concepts is enough to help you and your team members begin to have conversations about what matters most to them and what energizes them. Taking the time to really get to know each person you are working with will make the next steps much easier and will make you a better leader in general.

Chapter Highlights

As we discussed earlier, leveraging energy is something you do with people, not to them. For you to generate real commitment from other people, they first have to agree that the change is good for them (based on their passions). Secondly, they need to consciously wrap their heads around the change initiative and agree to go forward with the proposed approach (mindsets). Finally, they need to activate their hands (styles) to make the change a reality.

The next chapters will help you use what you now know about your team members' internal energy to help you connect and communicate in a way that leads to genuine commitment.

"If there is any one secret of success,
it lies in the ability to get the other person's point of view
and see things from his angle as well as from your own."
~ Henry Ford

9

Connecting and Communicating

Once you have identified the elements of energy that are core to each person, your next task is to promote openness to change. How do you this? By connecting with what each person cares about! When you interact with each person, you have the opportunity to connect your message to their own sources of energy.

Step 2 of the Change at the Core process is to connect and communicate to promote openness to change.

Connecting with People Based on Styles

Because style is the most observable element of internal energy, it is easiest to deduce. As you read this book, you probably thought about the people you work with and formed some hypotheses about their styles.

Once you know a person's natural style, you can increase your chances of connecting with him/her by making a deliberate effort to use the words that energize him/her.

People with this style...	Are energized by words like...
Driving	Results
Influencing	Point of View
Steady	Trust
Careful	Details

In addition to using the "trigger words" described above, you can tailor your approach to each person to increase the likelihood that your message will resonate with him/her. We've provided some tips for doing so on the following pages. Remember, the intent of sharing these tips is not to encourage manipulation or deception. Rather, the intent is for you to be able to connect with each person so that you can have meaningful discussions.

Driving Style

1. When planning to communicate with people who have a Driving Style, keep in mind that:

   - They have a very short attention span.

   - They are quick thinking and action-oriented decision makers.

   - Speed and responsiveness are rewarded by this group.

2. Discuss the benefits of your proposition first. If you delay expressing the benefits, you will lose or annoy them.

3. Answer the question, "What's in it FOR ME?" Once they get this, their minds will begin to churn, seeking ways to use your proposal to their advantage.

4. Let them know they are in charge because people with this style want to drive the process. Let them make the decision on how to proceed, and they will—quickly.

Influencing Style

1. When planning to communicate with people who have an Influencing Style, keep in mind that:

    • They have a slightly longer attention span than the D's.

    • Being optimistic, they will quickly see the benefits, opportunities, or upside to your proposal for the group.

    • Proactive approaches are rewarded by this group.

2. As you discuss your proposal, include them in the dialogue. They want to feel that their voice and perspectives are heard and that they in turn might influence the decision. Be prepared for a longer conversation, because people with this style like to talk it out.

3. Answer the question, "What's in it FOR US, the team?" Once they get this, their minds will begin to churn, seeking ways to use your proposal to their team's advantage.

4. Let them know you value their opinion and welcome them as champions for your efforts. They will actually help you sell your ideas internally to the decision-makers and to the troops at large. Simply ask for their support and together determine what it will take to enlist them in your cause.

Steady Style

1. When planning to communicate with people who have a Steady Style, keep in mind that:

   - They have a progressively longer attention span than the D's and I's.

   - They are cautious. They want to know they can "trust" that you have done this work before and that it was successfully completed.

   - They will want a list of references AND they will check them out.

2. As you discuss your proposal, include a high-level overview of the process or structure you will follow and discuss how you have already addressed these issues in the past.

3. Answer the question, "What's in it FROM US, the team? What will we be asked to do in order to succeed in this venture?" Once this group understands where you want to go and why, the members will trust you and be more open to your suggestions and recommendations.

4. You must also let them know that you want to work in partnership or collaboration with them to complete the mission. After you get through their barriers, they will be a good reference for others whom you will need to recruit to achieve your objective.

Careful Style

1. When planning to communicate with people who have a Careful Style, keep in mind that:

    *   They have a very long attention span—they'll stay with you all day to be sure their detailed questions are answered.

    *   Being pessimistic, they will ask a lot of tough questions and seek to play the devil's advocate.

    *   These people have extremely high standards of perfection that must be met to their satisfaction. They are often the evaluators of your proposals or gatekeepers of the status.

2. The style of these people causes them to see the holes in any plan. This means that they will constantly be looking for the fatal flaw in your presentation. This characteristic serves them well in their role in life—to follow established rules and procedures, and to understand and express the consequences of non-compliance.

3. Answer the question, "What's in it FROM ME? What will I now have to do in order to implement your proposal or directive and what 'problems' will that potentially cause?"

4. Let them know that you value their high standards and welcome the opportunity to meet their stringent requirements. Once you do meet their standards, they will support your efforts and proposals.

Connecting to All Styles

We were working with an organization that was in the midst of an industry consolidation. Through a series of mergers and acquisitions, one unique piece of the business had stayed intact, but had been shuffled from one acquiring company to another over the course of a 36-month period. Our client was about to sell this piece of the business one more time. Their primary concern was how to react to the negativism that was sure to be expressed by the group's leaders and employees about yet another change in ownership, direction and approach.

We were hired to teach the transition team how to break the news to these confused and disgruntled stakeholders and to do it in a way that allowed them to see the benefits of being a part of the new acquiring company's vast network. There were only two things the transition team could be sure of: (1) they didn't know the styles of their audience members so they had to appeal to all styles simultaneously; and (2) the attendees would probably be hostile to the messengers.

The transition team's spokesperson started the presentation without introducing herself or the rest of the team, primarily because the audience didn't really care who they were. They were totally focused on their own individual situations and simply wanted to stone whoever took the stage. The spokesperson's introductory presentation went something like this.

"Today you're going to learn about (1) a change that will stabilize our business; (2) how this change in ownership will provide continuity for future growth and development; and (3) how to leverage this new distribution system with far greater benefits than the one we have now." In these few words, she got the attention of all the Drivers in the room. These are the folks who only care about the results and getting directly to the bottom line. They naturally have a very short fuse and attention span. They want to know what's in it "FOR ME."

Next, she moved to address the Influencers in the crowd. "Let me ask you a question: If you could finally land a home where the parent company really valued this piece of business, how might that impact your business?" As the answers came from the audience, the stressful energy began to subside. The transition team now had the attention of the Influencers, who let their imagination run wild by describing their highly desired future state and what it would mean to their individual businesses. What's in it "FOR US" became clearer.

Once this was concluded, the transition team presented the history of the acquiring firm. The spokesperson talked about the firm's strategic vision, presented evidence of the employees' passion for this business, and laid out a high-level map of the transition plan and timeline. She also talked about the firm's successes in implementing such changes and provided references. This was exactly what most of the audience wanted to hear. In doing so, she connected with all the Steady people in the room. These folks wanted to trust that the new organization's processes and procedures would be good for them. According to their style, they wanted to know what's in it "FROM US"—what will we have to do in the future to be successful.

Finally, she moved to the Careful people. These folks will generally challenge the status quo unless they have a compelling reason to change—namely that the current system is broken and that delaying change is not an option for survival. While this group generally makes up the smallest portion of the audience, they can vocally and emotionally derail the change process by finding the fatal flaw in any situation. Actually, this critical view is their gift. If the transition team could answer all of their questions, they too would come on board. The challenge was to keep the presentation on track without derailing the agenda to address questions before all the facts were presented.

The spokesperson said, "As we go into more detail about the change in ownership and what it will mean to you, please feel free to ask us anything. If, for the sake of time, we can't answer your questions from the front of the room, we will meet with you individually afterward to answer all your questions." Now here's the thing—left to their own devices, the Careful Style group would never run out of questions and concerns. In a high-level roll out presentation like this, the transition team couldn't allow these folks to ask too many questions if they were to get through their timed agenda. But they made it okay for the Careful folks to ask the questions. They were now satisfied to listen first and ask questions later. This is important because people with this style need to know what's in it "FROM ME" personally.

By using this approach, the transition team's spokesperson actually connected with the entire audience in about 15 minutes. She then turned the presentation over to other experts to go into greater depth, knowing that the audience would be engaged in the learning process. They were all in a place where they could listen to the messages that they might not have heard when they originally walked into the room. So why did we coach the transition team to take this approach when introducing the unpopular change? First, this change was NOT an option. The decision to sell this portion of the business operation had already been consummated. Second, the acquiring company did indeed believe that this piece of the operations would be profitable and productive for them. Third, the team had to get the audience members out of their current state of fear, fatigue, uncertainty, and doubt and into a more open, thoughtful state to hear the messages that would impact their future. This simple approach of appealing to all behavior styles worked in this instance.

Connecting with People Based on Passions

While connecting and communicating with people based on their styles is useful, connecting and communicating based on passions is even more powerful.

As we discussed earlier, our passions indicate what we are drawn toward and what we move away from. Being able to connect with people around the things that energize and motivate them at their deepest subconscious level may mean the difference between indifference, rejection, and wholehearted commitment.

In Chapter 5, you read the details of the six passions. As a reminder, the table below summarizes the trigger words for each passion. On the following page, you'll see an example of how one leader learned to connect with people's passions.

People with a Passion for...	Are energized by words like...
Knowledge	Learn, Understand, Curious, Know, Deeper Meaning, Smart, Wise, Analyze
Results	Practical, Productive, ROI, Useful, Earn, Achieve, Invest, Bottom Line
Creativity	Create, Harmony, Balance, Appreciation, Work/Life, Time to Reenergize
People	Help, Serve, Contribute, Teach, Coach, Humanity, Connect, Volunteer, People
Leading	Lead, Be #1, The Best, Energetic, Distinctive, Excel, Power
Tradition	Standards, Discipline, Protocol, Stability, Beliefs, Routines, Sacrifice

Connecting Based on Passions

When two industry giants merged, integration teams from each of the legacy organizations were chartered to work together to address the concerns of the SEC, which was overseeing the merger.

When the two integration teams came together to discuss the SEC requirements, disagreements about how to proceed quickly surfaced. In our work with the teams, we helped them identify the passions that their organizations had been founded on. It became clear that one of the legacy companies embodied Passion for Results. It was known for being quick to market. The leadership team cherished responsiveness and empowered employees to act quickly. The other equally successful legacy firm had flourished based on a Passion for Tradition. Its employees were slower to act, prided themselves on flawless execution by following the intent of the law, and ran every decision up the management chain before finalizing a decision.

Once the teams understood each other's perspective, they were able to combine the best of both organizations to deliver timely and accurate data to gain SEC approval in a smooth and seamless way. In fact, the new chairman said, "Our integration teams performed above and beyond our expectations. It is hard to believe how much they accomplished in such a short timeframe." Passion recognition and alignment made all the difference in this instance.

Chapter Highlights

For your change initiative to succeed, connecting and communicating with your team is essential. Tapping into each person's style, passion, and mindset will help ensure that you are connecting.

Promote openness to change by connecting with what each person cares about!

"The only way on earth to influence the other fellow
is to talk about what he wants and show him how to get it."

~ Dale Carnegie

10

Understanding and Addressing Resistance

Now that you have connected and communicated with each person and/or group, you may think your work is done. It's tempting to believe that a great motivational speech or a persuasive conversation are all you need to make people feel committed enough to drive change. In reality, it rarely happens that way.

> "It is a terrible thing to look over your shoulder when you are
> trying to lead—and find no one there."
> ~ Franklin Delano Roosevelt

The initial conversations we discussed in the last chapter were designed to promote openness—not to seal the deal. Now your job is to understand and respond to each person's level of acceptance or resistance.

Surfacing Resistance

A great deal has been written about overcoming resistance. We believe that approaching resistance as something that needs to be "overcome" is precisely the wrong thing to do.

As we discussed earlier, many leaders make the mistake of believing that they are driving change. These leaders often get frustrated by the roadblocks and speed bumps they encounter, and they attempt to steamroller right over anyone who resists their change initiative.

Step 3 of the Change at the Core process is to understand, appreciate, and address resistance.

*Overpowering resistance
doesn't reduce problems,
it simply hides them.*

In reality, overpowering resistance doesn't reduce problems, it simply hides them. And hidden problems are like time bombs just waiting to explode and destroy all the work that has gone into your change effort.

Therefore, we advocate doing everything you can to use your initial conversations (Step 2) to launch more intensive and meaningful conversations that are specifically designed to draw out resistance. When you find out what is not working, what concerns people have, and where the problems may be and when you respect and appreciate what people have to say, you'll find that you are far more likely to generate commitment and solutions.[22]

One way to view resistance is to look at it from the perspective of what people are doing to impede your change. Instead, we view resistance as a helpful clue. The degree of resistance we encounter indicates whether or not we have built support for our change.

Levels of Resistance

Rick Maurer is an expert on change and resistance. According to Maurer, there are three levels of resistance to change:[23]

Level 1: "I don't understand it."

Level 2: "I don't like it."

Level 3: "I don't like you."

Level 1 resistance involves information: facts, figures, and ideas. It is the world of thinking and rational action, presentations, diagrams, and logical arguments. Level 1 resistance may come from:

- Lack of information

- Disagreement with data

- Lack of exposure to critical information

- Confusion over what it means

Many leaders make the mistake of treating all resistance as if it were Level 1. They hold more meetings and make more PowerPoint presentations when, in fact, something completely different is often called for.

Level 2 is an emotional reaction to the change that is based on fear. People are afraid that this change will cause them to lose face, status, control—maybe even their jobs.

Level 3 resistance is rooted in distrust. It is highly unlikely that we will generate commitment from people who don't like and trust us. Maurer writes, "When the people you are trying to influence feel that you are using spin, they get suspicious and begin to analyze what it was that you might have meant when you spoke. They no longer accept what you say at face-value."[24]

Understanding Resistance

Research on change shows that people support change when they:

- Trust the person/people leading the change

- Recognize the problem that prompted change

- Feel a sense of urgency to address the problem

- Understand the solution being proposed

- Agree the solution being proposed makes sense for the organization

- Believe they will play a meaningful part in implementing the change

- Believe the people leading the change have a well-thought-out plan and believe that the plan is working

- Accept the personal loss that accompanies the change

Essentially, resistance is the opposite of support. People resist change when they:

- Don't trust the person/people leading the change

- Don't recognize the problem that prompted change

- Don't feel a sense of urgency to address the problem

- Don't understand the solution being proposed

- Disagree with the solution being proposed and believe another solution makes more sense for the organization

- Don't believe they will play a meaningful part in implementing the change

- Believe the people leading the change have not thought out the plans for implementation or they don't see that the plan could work

- Are not willing or able to accept the personal loss that accompanies the change

For the most part, each of these factors fit into a natural hierarchy. For example, trust is first because trust is at the foundation of support and a lack of trust is the most difficult element of resistance to remedy.

To help you understand, appreciate, and address resistance, we've created a tool for you on the next page. Take a few moments now to think of a specific change you are leading and the people you are working with to implement the change.

Tool: Understanding Support and Resistance

Write the initials of your team members and/or key stakeholders in the shaded boxes across the top of the chart. Use a scale of 1 to 5 to indicate the degree to which you believe the statements below are TRUE for each person. When you are not sure, or cannot make a determination, use a question mark.

Strongly Disagree	Disagree	Partly Agree Partly Disagree	Agree	Strongly Agree	Don't Know/NA
1	**2**	**3**	**4**	**5**	**?**

1. Trusts the person/people leading the change					
2. Recognizes the problem that prompted change					
3. Feels a sense of urgency to address the problem					
4. Understands the solution being proposed					
5. Agrees the solution being proposed makes sense for the organization					
6. Believes he/she will play a meaningful part in implementing the change					
7. Believes the people leading the change have a well-thought-out plan					
8. Accepts the personal loss that accompanies the change					

Once you have finished, take a look back at your chart. Do you have a lot of question marks? That's not unusual. In fact, we often find that change leaders who are encountering resistance have not had enough meaningful conversations to gauge the root of the resistance.

Low scores may seem discouraging, but they are actually helpful clues. Low scores indicate areas where you can use your influence to build more support. Understanding people's passions, styles, and mindsets can help in all of these areas. Let's look at how.

Factor #1: Trust

While there are many factors that build and destroy trust, a key component is the alignment of values between two people. As we discussed earlier, there are six primary values (we call them passions) and people vary widely in terms of their prioritization of each. When you share a value/passion with someone, you feel confident that he/she will make the same decisions you would. Therefore you trust that person more.

So does this mean that people never trust those who have passions that are different from their own? No. In these cases, we have found that trust can still be formed as long as both people's actions are still predictable. I may value people and my boss may value results. It is still possible for me to trust my boss because at some level I know I can count on him to make decisions to put results first. So the key here is not to pretend to be someone you are not, or to try to "fake" your style or passion.

The best route is to be authentic, honest, and consistent and to take the time to build relationships with others before attempting to engage them in change.

Factors #2 and #3: Recognition of the Problem/Feeling a Sense of Urgency

We've combined these next two factors because while separate, they are related. People need to recognize a problem and feel a sense of urgency about addressing it in order to be committed to finding a solution.

Recent research by John Kotter has indicated that these two factors are often overlooked in poorly implemented change efforts. Many times change leaders charge into situations with a focus on a particular solution. They overlook the fact that people do not "buy" solutions unless they feel that a) they have a problem in the first place; and b) the problem is urgent.[25]

Many leaders spend a great deal of time gathering information about the market, competitors, the economy, and so on. They also study internal metrics until they can recite the stock price, number of product lines, and time to market in their sleep. They are intimately familiar with the data that are compelling change. Not only that, they usually come up with a plan for moving their organization forward. They know both the problem and the solution. So what do they do? They hold a town hall meeting, and with great fanfare and enthusiasm announce the VISION FOR THE FUTURE. What do they get? Blank stares. Panicked looks. Rolling eyes. Not everyone in the organization feels the sense of urgency they do! The problem is that they know the full story, but no one else does. In their employees' minds, they have jumped to a solution when there is no problem.

To get people to embrace a change, you must start with getting them to recognize the need for a change in the first place.

On the other hand, Maurer found that in 95 percent of successful changes, most stakeholders saw a compelling need for the change.[26] They understood the risk of doing nothing. Therefore, to get people to embrace a change, you must start with getting them to recognize the need for a change in the first place.

We like to the use the analogy of a fire when talking about building a sense of urgency. People need to feel the heat in order to put out a fire. It's up to us as leaders to light a fire in our organizations in order to jump-start the change process. But remember, you need to light a fire within people, not under them. Overdoing scare tactics can cause people to feel threatened. Threat can cause paralysis and panic. Workplace psychologist Bob Rosen has coined a term for finding the right balance of emotions. He calls this "just enough anxiety."[27] At this point, you may already recognize that each person's internal energy is pivotal when it comes to problem recognition and feeling a sense of urgency. Our internal energy elements greatly influence the factors that we tune into and those we tune out. Someone who has a Passion for Results may feel just enough anxiety to act if his bonus is at risk. Someone with a Passion for Tradition may feel just enough anxiety when her stability is threatened.

Again, understanding your people will help you understand which messages will help you create a sense of urgency.

Getting It at a Gut Level

A few years ago, we worked with a technology company on the roll-out of its new brand. We'd been asked to develop a training class that explained the new brand position. The changes that we were about to introduce would impact the work of every person in the company. There were new guidelines about how to talk to customers, new rules about how to use the logo and brand icons, and a new color palette for use in everything from external marketing to internal documents.

Any of you who have worked with high-tech companies know that the best way to kill an idea is that say that, "corporate says we have to do it this way." How in the world could we get 7,000 "techies" to not only comply with the brand guidelines, but to want to? We knew that we needed every person to understand at a gut level why brand consistency, and therefore guidelines, were needed. So we started our program with a visual tour of some great brands—Apple, Starbucks, Ann Taylor, and Disney. We got people interacting and talking about why each brand was so recognizable. Time and time again, the audience saw that deliberate, consistent use of fonts, colors, and shapes helped to create a strong brand.

Next, we showed slides that compared and contrasted all of the advertising and marketing this company had been doing. Without us having to say a word, the audience members realized that their old brand was in complete chaos. We ran more than 70 of these sessions, and every single time, this was a pivotal moment. You could watch people sit up and almost immediately become willing participants in the change process instead of prisoners in a training class.

Factor #4: Understanding the Solution

Once people recognize the problem and feel a sense of urgency to solve it, they need to understand the solution being proposed. One phenomenon that we have observed over the years is that "understanding" is very different for people with different styles.

People with Dialed-Up D and Dialed-Up I styles focus on the big picture. They are often content with knowing the vision or picture of the future. Too many details bore and de-energize them. When one of these people says, "I don't understand" a proposed solution, he/she usually means, "I can't picture the end result" and/or "I don't know why we are making this change."

Conversely, people with Dialed-Up S and C styles care little about the big picture. They want the details behind how a change will work. Hearing "I don't understand" from one of these people translates into, "I don't see a step-by-step plan for this."

In any case, when someone tells you that they don't understand a change, don't launch into a long technical monologue. Chances are they understand the literal words you have used, but don't understand what it means for them and from them.

A key to addressing resistance is plugging back into people's passions.

Factor #5: Agreeing with the Solution

People may understand your solution, but still not agree with it. Passions are key here. People will have a hard time being motivated to go against their values. A key to addressing resistance is plugging back into people's passions. If you are driven by one passion and someone is resisting because he/she is driven by another, instead of positioning one value (passion) as winning out over another, look for ways to explore alternatives that support both. Invite discussion by using phrases such as:

- How can we stay in the black during this recession (Passion for Results) and avoid laying people off (Passion for People)?

- How can we look for innovative solutions (Passion for Creativity) and remain true to the products our customers have come to rely on (Passion for Tradition)?

The story below illustrates how one group was able to plug into passions to look for a way out of what seemed like a hopeless situation.

Plugging into Passions

A marketing and sales organization was historically growing its net income at a rate of 6 percent a year. Unfortunately, the market indicators showed that a slowdown in its industry and the industries it sold into was about to occur. In a meeting with the CEO of the parent company, employees projected net income to be flat at $75 million in the coming year. They saw this as a stretch objective given the gloomy forecast by the industry experts.

Upon hearing this, the CEO sat up straight in his chair and said, "Seventy-five million! Walking into this room I intended to tell you that a 6 percent growth rate isn't good enough. Within three years I expect you to contribute $200 million in net income to our enterprise." Jaws dropped as the CEO left the room. One person after another asked, "Where did he get that number? Did he pull it out of the air?" The organization stewed for about a month.

The senior executives then called together 200 members from around the world to decide what to do about this $200 million bogey. Based on their previous interactions with this group, the meeting designers guessed that the top three passions for almost every member of the group were Passion for (1) Results, (2) Leading, and (3) Knowledge.

With this information, the meeting facilitators designed a three-day workshop. As the group convened, the lead facilitator asked the group, "If we could do one thing to get us closer to the $200 million target, what would that one thing be?" After a dead silence, the facilitator said, "Let me ask this question in a different way: If we could learn what causes growth in our sector [Knowledge] and if we could use this knowledge to develop a world-class business unit [Leading], what would one thing be that we could we do to get closer to the $200 million prize [Results]?"

Surprising as it may seem, one idea slowly surfaced after another. A list of 25 ideas was generated and then culled down to the 10 that could have the most impact. The group was split into sub-teams of 20 volunteers each to begin to work on the idea that they felt (1) the most energy toward; or (2) the one they felt they could positively impact the most. One of the outputs from their work together was a high-level estimate of the dollar impact related to their area of focus. When all was tallied, the organization leaders felt that they could move from $75 million to $125 million within three years. While this was far short of the goal, it gave the group members hope that they could at least move the needle forward.

This organization worked extremely hard and engaged its entire workforce in this initiative. In every internal communication (newsletters, meetings, presentations, updates, conferences, etc.) and in every external publication (annual report, editorials, advertisements, tradeshows, etc.) leaders spoke in terms of their passion for Knowledge, Leading, and Getting Results. The message resonated across the board because it was congruent with the energy they put forth.

The end of the story is this: The organization did NOT achieve the $200 million goal at the end of year three—the goal was actually achieved at the end of year two! Along the way, leaders stumbled into a market that no other division was selling into. As Louis Pasteur once said, "Chance favors the prepared mind."

Factor #6: A Meaningful Part to Play

As we alluded to earlier, a key factor that determines people's commitment to a change effort is the degree to which they feel they have, or will have, a meaningful way to contribute.

In Chapter 11, we'll cover the specifics of unleashing energy. While doing this step is important, it is equally important to tell people that they have a key role long before you expect them to jump into action.

A Cog in a Wheel or a Pivotal Part?

For years, we've worked on projects for a large defense contracting company. Like many others in the industry, this company has evolved dramatically over the past 15 years. In 2001, the company stood up a new sector made up of 18,000 employees from 16 different companies that had all been acquired over a short period of time. As you can imagine, getting 18,000 employees on the same ERP system, the same benefits program, and the same pension plan was a nightmare.

Add to that the challenge of getting everyone in the sector to work together, to collaborate, and to stop thinking of each other as competitors. Anxiety was running high and employee retention was running low.

When we listened to employees and frontline managers, we heard again and again that people were feeling disconnected and disengaged. Imagine yourself in their shoes. You work for a small software development firm with 50 employees, many of whom are your best friends. You are bought by a firm with 2,000 employees. A year later you are acquired by a company with 6,000 on the payroll. Before you know it your firm has merged with a company that has 18,000 employees worldwide. In the span of three years, you've gotten five mugs. You are single handedly clothing a community with the company T-shirts that have gone to Goodwill. You feel like a number, not a name.

We recognized that the pride employees had felt in their start-ups had been replaced with estrangement. When customers asked what was up with all of the acquisitions, employees would say, "I have no idea—I guess they are trying to take over the world or something."

What most employees hadn't been taught was the reason for all of the growth and rapid-fire acquisitions. So we set out to get everyone on the same page.

We knew we needed more transparency, so among other things, we embarked on a plan to train all of the frontline managers about how the company had been organized and why. We showed video clips and shared Fortune magazine articles about the company's evolution. We let audiences know that they had been brought into the organization to fulfill a vision that the president had defined over a decade earlier. We drew a wall-size fishbone diagram showing the mergers and acquisitions that had taken place over the past five years and asked each person to add their names to the timeline. We talked about the value that each small company brought with it and how each acquisition was helping the overall company realize the vision.

The change in the atmosphere that came about from communicating the vision and emphasizing every company's and every person's part in it was palpable! Each person now saw that he/she and his/her peers had a meaningful part to play.

Factor #7: Believing in the Plan/Feeling the Plan is Working

Even if people don't resist a change at the beginning, attitudes will shift if it begins to look as if the initiative is falling apart or losing momentum. Most employees have seen too many fads and failed change initiatives over the course of their working lives. It is difficult for them to stay personally committed when plans disintegrate into chaos.

Sometimes the people who seem to be the most resistant are the ones who truly wanted change most in the first place. If change fails or doesn't seem to be happening, these folks can become disillusioned.

> "If you scratch a cynic, you'll find a disappointed idealist."
> —George Carlin

While you want your team members to take ownership for change and to drive change themselves, remember not to abandon them. Take the time to check in to find out where the barriers are and commit to helping your team overcome obstacles that could stall progress.

In fact, when working with organizations on a change effort or initiative, we like to ask employees to use the "driving" metaphor to describe what it feels like to be in the middle of the change. Here are some of the descriptions we've heard:

"It's like bumper cars. Everyone is running into each other."

"I think it's like a demolition derby. We're just destroying everything that worked."

"To me it feels like the parkway at 5 p.m. in rush hour. Stop and go. Make a bit of progress, and then sit around and wait."

"I feel like I am driving without a destination and without a map. No one is telling me what the priorities are or what's expected of me."

Exploring the metaphors of people who are in the middle of the change can help us be better change leaders. When we recognize that we aren't driving, we can begin to see ourselves as being in the position of planning, directing, and facilitating the journey for others.

Factor #8: Accepting Personal Loss

In the 1980s William Bridges coined the term "organizational transition" and authored many books and articles that helped countless leaders address the people side of change.[28]

One of Bridges' most cited models concerns the psychological phases that people experience when going through a transition. Thanks to Bridges, we now understand that almost every change involves loss. People affected by a change may be losing a range of things including:

- Power

- Status

- Relationships

- Comfort

- Choice

To lead change, we must be able to help people accept loss. At the same time, we can also look for ways to minimize loss where possible.

To lead change, we must be able to help people accept loss. At the same time, we can also look for ways to minimize loss where possible.

What's important to realize is that different people will be more affected by different losses, depending on what's at their core. For example, someone with a Careful Style will likely resist a loss of control. On the other hand, someone with the Influencing Style may not be bothered by a loss in control, but may be devastated at the prospect of losing relationships.

Passions play an extremely powerful role here as well. A change that threatens a person's motivation is a hard change to accept.

People with a Passion for...	Feel loss a sense of loss from ...
Knowledge	No ability to learn Shallow work Nothing to learn—Everything is understood
Results	Wasted resources No interest in ROI Seniority-based incentives
Creativity	Lack of harmony Stifled creativity Workaholic environment
People	Self-promotion Non-people focus Downsizing
Leading	One of many Stagnation Micromanaged
Tradition	Freewheeling organization No rules Everyone for him/herself

There are many different models that represent how individuals react to change. Generally, most researchers agree that people's reactions to change follow a curve and that curve can be divided into stages.

- Stage 1 is characterized by shock and denial. During this phase, people may say things like, "I don't understand." Don't be fooled into thinking more information is going to help at this point. This is an emotional reaction, not an intellectual one.

- In Stage 2, people have moved beyond shock and are now experiencing what we call, "The Valley of FFUD." FFUD stands for fear, fatigue, uncertainty, and doubt.

- Stage 3 starts with understanding and then progresses to acceptance and moving on.

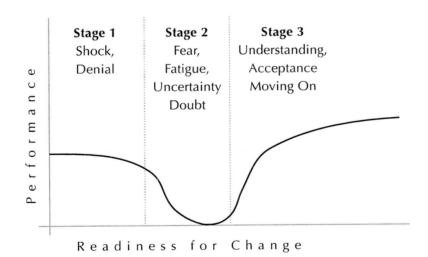

We like to use this model to help leaders understand where people are in terms of their readiness to change and what they need to do to help people move through the stages. If people on your team or people you need to influence are at Stage 1 or Stage 2, it is impossible to force them to jump ahead to Stage 3 (understanding and acceptance). Instead of trying to figure out how to get people to immediately buy into a change, your job is to help them move through the change curve.

The key to using this model is understanding that:

a) Different people will be in different stages at any given time;

b) You must lead each person based on where he/she is—not where you are; and

c) You can facilitate movement through the phases—but you cannot force or rush it.

Why Individuals React Differently to the Same Change

While we find this model and others like it to be very useful, it can also oversimplify reactions to change. As our colleague, Bruce Hogge says, "All models are wrong, but most models are useful."

What we have found is that not everyone goes through all three stages every time. Consider this: If the change was your idea, you may never experience Stages 1 and 2. On the other hand, if we are attempting to introduce a change that requires a significant shift in a person's mindsets or, more importantly, one that violates a person's core passions, we can expect him/her to experience the whole gamut of emotional reactions to change.

As human beings, when we first face ANY change in our lives (new organization, new assignment, new teammate, etc.), our subconscious minds invoke the Pleasure/Pain principle. We ask ourselves:

- Will this change bring me pleasure or pain?

- Will this change be good for me or bad for me?

- Will this change make me happy or sad?

What can you do if you are asking people to make a leap that might hurt?

If we perceive the change as being good for us, it's easy to commit ourselves and our resources to seeing it through. Alternatively, if we see the change as being harmful to us to any degree, our resistance will kick in.

Ultimately what this means for you is that if you are seeing signs of shock, denial, fear, fatigue, uncertainty, or doubt then this is a clue that people are feeling the change will be harmful to them.

So what can you do if you are asking people to make a leap that might hurt?

Push, Pull, or Power?

In talking about addressing resistance, we often use the analogy of teaching a child to jump off a diving board for the first time. The child may be standing at the edge, terrified. You could walk up behind him and push him off. Chances are that if you try this, you'll severely damage his trust in you. You could swim beneath him and beg or plead for him to jump off. This approach could take forever and be very frustrating for both of you. Your other alternative is to tap into the child's internal energy to help him find the personal power to commit to the jump and to follow through. Perhaps he wants to be able to play with the big kids. Perhaps he wants you to know he can come to the pool without your supervision. Perhaps he dreams of doing back flips and belly flops. Plugging into what he wants is the only way for him to feel good about this first jump.

Think about it. When you lead change, do you typically try to push or plead? Wouldn't it be incredible to be able to power change instead? That is Change at the Core.

Change at the Core helps you power change instead of pushing it or pleading for it.

Chapter Highlights

As we covered the major causes of resistance in this chapter, we linked ways of understanding and addressing resistance to people's internal energy. We did this not to encourage you to be manipulative. Instead, we are hoping to provide the tools for you to truly understand what is happening in the heads and hearts of the people you are counting on. As the saying goes, "Seek first to understand before you seek to be understood."

When you understand your people and you have built a trusting relationship with them, they are much more likely to work with you to effect change—even if they don't particularly like change itself or the exact change being proposed.

"Resistance is not the primary reason why changes fail.
The real problem is that leaders plan and instigate major changes
in ways that create inertia, apathy, and opposition."
~ Rick Maurer, author of *Beyond the Wall of Resistance*

11

Unleashing Each Person's Energy to Power Change

The final step in the Change at the Core process is to align and unleash each person's energy to power change. For many leaders, this is the most exciting part. Individuals have been engaged and are now committed. When the leader can match responsibilities to energy, amazing progress can be made in a short period of time!

The keys to aligning and unleashing energy are:

- Plugging into Passions

- Managing Mindsets

- Leveraging Styles

Plugging into Passions

By now you are aware that passion is at the very core of internal energy. Our passions drive our actions and determine what motivates and demotivates us. It should therefore come as no surprise that the most powerful way to unleash energy is to plug into a person's passions.

The chart below reminds us of the passions that drive each person on our teams.

The final step of the Change at the Core process is to align and unleash each person's energy to power change.

The most powerful way to unleash energy is to plug into a person's passions.

When you can match responsibilities to energy, amazing progress can be made in a short period of time!

People with a Passion for...	Are Driven by...
Knowledge	Intellectual curiosity and the need to understand
Results	ROI and the need to get results
Creativity	Harmony and the need to achieve balance
People	The need to help others
Leading	The need to lead
Tradition	The need to maintain high standards and controls

The example below illustrates the way that one team deliberately plugged into passions when forming a change team.

Unleashing Passions

A mid-cap organization was in the process of going through an organizational renewal. As part of their integrated effort, employees completed a thorough review of the computer technology that supported their operating, support, and infrastructure needs. After fully defining both their current state and future state needs, the Executive Leadership Team (ELT) chartered a small cross-functional group of four employees to design the computer technology (hardware and software) that would lead the organization into the future. Team members were selected based on their primary and secondary areas of passion.

The initiative team was lead by Larry, a business executive who had a Passion for Leading and Results. As a team leader, Larry focused on ensuring that this team determined solutions that would give them standing with their customers, employees, and competitors. Their technological approach also had to increase their market share, be cost effective, and meet the needs of the businesses they supported.

Jackie, a senior computer analyst, was a natural for the team. She was selected for her Passion for Knowledge and Tradition. Jackie prided herself on keeping up with leading-edge technologies. She was part of a vast network of technical experts around the world who communicated continuously about the latest and greatest in the technology arena. Maintaining high standards of operations was another of Jackie's key objectives—driven by her Passion for Tradition.

Phyllis, a sales executive with a penchant for graphic design, brought a Passion for Creativity to the team. Phyllis knew how to draw attention to products and services in the marketplace. The team relied on her to communicate the benefits of their recommendations in a way that showed their applicability both internally with employees and externally with customers and suppliers.

Henry, a financial executive with a Passion for Results and People, rounded out the team. Henry was charged with evaluating the various technology scenarios to find the one or ones that would have the greatest impact on the bottom line. As the team moved through implementation, he was also on point for managing the internal communications strategy and training on the new technology to ensure a high adoption rate.

In the team meeting that kicked off this effort, the executive champions from the ELT presented a high-level charter for this initiative, the reasons each member was picked for the team, and the roles and responsibilities of each. They also noted that they would be available

Leaders often need to help people channel known strengths in a new direction with a new mindset.

for informal guidance reviews and would act as initiative champions for any presentations the team would subsequently make to the ELT.

The energy of this team for the IT initiative was incredibly high simply because each member was selected based on his/her intrinsic passions. They hit the ground running. When unforeseen challenges or roadblocks arose, the team came together to resolve them with a singleness of purpose. Their work product was delivered and implemented on time and 20 percent under budget. Only minor tweaks were needed in the first few weeks after implementation.

Managing Mindsets

A second critical element of aligning and unleashing energy is managing mindsets. For success in any situation, it is paramount to clearly design team member roles based on the "ideal" styles, passions, and mindsets to achieve the desired outcomes within your organization. When the situation and/or roles change, leaders need to take time to explicitly realign expectations. Often this involves helping people channel known strengths in a new direction with a new mindset.

Managing Mindsets

We were working with a group of executives in a highly technical field. These people had been born and bred to exhibit introverted behavior. Up until this point in their careers, they had always been tasked to pore through tons of data to uncover either a unique solution to an existing problem or a fatal flaw in a proposed solution in their area of specialty. These folks were rewarded over and over again for being "super analysts" who focused on the task in front of them and who worked alone.

Ultimately these analysts were rewarded for their technical expertise by being promoted to the executive ranks. Now they were required to spend more time working with people, coaching their staff, making quick and intuitive decisions, and building relationships with their customers. These are more extroverted "people" behaviors than the introverted "technical" behaviors of their past. So how do you think they performed? Their upward feedback was abysmal and their business performance suffered. This is a typical style conflict that repeats itself in organizations all over the world. These new, emerging leaders were now being asked to be less process- and task-focused and more people-focused—a shift that did not come naturally to many of them.

In our coaching sessions, we asked our clients to try several different approaches. First, we asked them to identify a role model for their executive position—someone they could study and learn from regarding people interactions. We also asked them to take some courses about people management and then consciously apply their lessons learned back on the job. Finally, to leverage their current style in their new jobs, we asked them to be very task- or mission-focused by setting up routines within their business day to specifically interact with others (customers and employees) on a scheduled basis. This meant that they had to consciously think about the outcomes or results they desired from their people interactions and maintain that focus for just brief periods of time throughout the day. Basically, this required a shift from a highly intense Process Mindset to more of a People Mindset. Once their mission was complete, they could return to their more comfortable introverted style while continuing to think about their people.

Leveraging Styles

Once you have aligned people with what energizes them by plugging into passions and channeled their energy by managing mindsets, you are ready to unleash their natural strengths. Assigning tasks according to each team member's inherent style allows you to do just that.

The chart on the next page shows some examples of how to match responsibilities to people's natural styles. The worksheets that follow enable you to start matching your own team members to tasks based on the strengths associated with their style.

Assigning tasks according to each team member's inherent style allows you to unleash their natural strengths.

Style	Best Fit Business Situations
↑D	• Crisis Mode • Quick Decision Needed • Tactical Decisions
↓D	• Long-Term, Strategic Decisions • Systematic Approach • Scoping and Defining a Problem
↑I	• Influencing and Persuading Others • Developing Strong Networks and Relationships • Motivating Others to Take Action
↓I	• Testing Capabilities • Evaluating Results • Negotiating Critical Concessions
↑S	• Completion is Essential • Calm in a Storm • Need for Planning and a Systematic Approach
↓S	• Multitasking • Brainstorming • Starting Initiatives
↑C	• Implementing Controls • Detailed Analysis • Finding Flaws
↓C	• Breaking Paradigms • Establishing New Rules and Roles • Taking a Global View

Style	Your Team Members	Ideas for Leveraging Their Strengths
↑ Dialed-Up D		
↔ Middle D		
Dialed-Down D ↓		
↑ Dialed-Up I		
↔ Middle I		
Dialed-Down I ↓		

Style	Your Team Members	Ideas for Leveraging Their Strengths
↑ Dialed-Up S		
←—→ Middle S		
Dialed-Down S ↓		
↑ Dialed-Up C		
←—→ Middle C		
Dialed-Down C ↓		

Unleashing Energy

Let's take a look at how one executive leveraged all of these elements recently to lead himself and his team through a change initiative.

New Mindset

A financial executive for a large international firm asked for our help in engaging his organization in an initiative focused on cost controls. We helped him shift his mindset from an emphasis on Processes to a consideration of the impact that cost controls would have on the People in the organization. The executive quickly realized that there is a huge distinction between "cost reduction" and "cost effectiveness." As he reflected on his colleagues and their styles and motivations, he realized that "cost reduction" efforts would be resisted. On the other hand, his colleagues would respond positively to getting the most VALUE for the cost. This one simple mindset shift allowed the executive to position his organization for a turnaround while maintaining his strong relationships with internal customers, vendors, and in some cases clients of his company.

Unleashing Passions

After the CFO shifted his own mindset to focus on people, he was ready to leverage the internal energy of his team to help with the company's cost effectiveness initiative. We reminded him of what drives people with differing passions and suggested ways that he could match assignments to passions:

Passion for Knowledge

Assign these people to research best practices both internally and externally, then choose the ones that will best fit in your specific organization.

Passion for Results

These employees will identify and negotiate cost versus value propositions, but they must understand that you are not cutting to the bone.

Passion for Creativity

These folks will be sure not to cut so deeply that you realize unintended consequences of your actions. They will provide balance in the recommendations offered.

Passion for People

Given the alternative of cutting operating costs or reducing people, these staff members will work hard to reduce the costs to save the people. Assign them to the people aspects of change.

Passion for Leading

Put these people on point to lead segments of your implementation plan.

Passion for Tradition

These people will be sure not to cut any corners that might put your organization at risk. Assign them to design your internal controls.

Leveraging Strengths

Finally, we reminded the CFO that when designing and implementing an action plan to make the needed changes, he actually needed folks with all four styles in order to develop a comprehensive approach. In initial meetings, the D's and I's will dominate the conversations as they tend to be the most verbal. In their effort to be quick to get their points recognized these folks go after the low-hanging fruit. The S's will sit back and think through the issues quietly, thinking about which of the brainstorm items can actually be implemented without causing undue harm. The C's will slow down the process by asking a ton of questions to be sure they fully understand each alternative and their related consequences. Given some time to think about it, the S's and C's will reach deep into the tree to come up with solutions that don't readily surface in initial brainstorming sessions. It's important to give them this time because this is where breakthrough solutions occur.

This triangulation of styles, passions, and mindsets is a great example of how to align, unleash, and channel energy.

Chapter Highlights

The keys to aligning and unleashing energy are:

- Plugging into Passions

- Managing Mindsets

- Leveraging Styles

"The needs of the team are best met
when we meet the needs of individual persons."
~ Max DePree

SECTION FOUR

Launching and Sustaining Change at the Core

"A leader leads by example, whether he wants to or not."
–Anonymous

12

Start with Your Own Core

At this point, we are hoping you are eager to start applying the ideas and techniques from Change at the Core. Before you do, however, remember that change begins with you. Taking the time to assess your own style, passion, and mindset is critical before you begin your work with others.

We encourage you to take a few moments to answer the questions below and to make an action plan for getting yourself in the mindset to lead successfully.

- What is your predominant style?

- What are your top two passions?

- What is your mindset currently focused on?

- What boosts your energy?

- What drains you?

- How do you react to change?

- How do you initiate/lead change?

- How will you develop, adapt, or partner with others to be more effective as a change leader?

Plugging into Your Passions

As you learned earlier, your passions are the most powerful force behind your decisions and actions. The very fact that you are reading a book on leading change indicates that you want to succeed. What else do you know about your passions? What are you driven by?

If, as you read this book and answered the questions on the previous page, you realized that you will need to demonstrate a new approach to leading change, remember to come back to why you are doing this in the first place. Your passions are what keep you motivated!

Shifting Your Mindset

In Chapter 6, we discussed the fact that every successful change initiative takes all mindsets into account. Often we find that the most important mindset to shift is that of the change leader.

Shifting a Mindset by Connecting with Passions

Bill is a senior leader we worked with recently. For his entire career, Bill's Driving Style and Passion for Leading were recognized and rewarded by his organization. He surrounded himself with the best and brightest "stars" and he rewarded them accordingly.

A new CEO/president took over Bill's company and quickly decided that there needed to be a significant culture shift. He and the HR organization made plans to change their reward system from recognizing star performance to one that would recognize team performance.

Bill openly displayed dissention against this change as "flavor of the month." While he did not explicitly sabotage team efforts, his communications and actions demonstrated an obvious lack of support. Internally, he could not wait until this initiative would pass.

The personal challenge for Bill escalated when the team initiative really took off. Support from both the top and bottom of the organizations was so strong that additional team initiatives began to sprout roots. Then one day, Bill's leader came to him. He told Bill that the company was about to undertake a significant change initiative that the executive board felt could really propel them beyond the competition. They named Bill to lead this change effort.

Now Bill had a decision to make. He could no longer fake it. He either had to get on board quickly and lead this change OR exit this bus at the next stop.

First, Bill looked inside himself to find his true passions. His Passion for Leading and his Passion for Results became the motivators for his change in mindset and attitude. For Bill to be successful, he knew that he would have to change his current perspectives around People, Processes, and Systems. He knew that he was now responsible for communicating the Systems perspective and convincing other People to join him.

The last point we'd like to make before we leave this topic is this: Nothing is more contagious than attitude!

Nothing is more contagious than attitude!

Recently we flew from Denver to Florida to deliver a program. On the flight home, the plane hit some bad turbulence. The sudden drops in altitude were some of the worst we have experienced in years. We gripped our armrests and reached for that little bag we all hope we'll never need. We glanced furtively around and saw other people doing the same. Everyone had looks of barely contained panic.

Suddenly, from about two rows in front of us, we heard a squeal of delight, and then another. A little girl of about three years old was laughing and giggling like she was on the world's best roller coaster!

Immediately the rest of the passengers started to relax. Each time the little girl squealed, everyone laughed. It started to feel like we were all on a ride and instead of feeling terrified, we felt just a bit of a thrill.

What does this example have to do with leading change? As we discussed in Chapter 1, most leaders find themselves in situations where they are responsible for implementing changes that others have conceived. The manner and attitude with which you approach a situation like this makes a huge difference when it is time for you to encourage others to commit. Your own attitude will be contagious to others. Manage your own mindset first.

Adapting Your Style

As part of your self-reflection, you may have recognized that you will need to adapt your own style at times in order to lead change successfully. Being able to adapt is an important leadership skill. Remember, however, that it may not be easy. You are naturally energized by certain behaviors. If you need to employ a different style, it is helpful to recognize that a) the shift is temporary and situational; and b) your flexibility will help you fulfill your own passions.

Many people find it helpful to use one of two techniques when they need to adapt: role modeling and routines. Each technique is described below.

Role Modeling

One way to learn to adapt your style is by modeling your behavior after someone whose success you would like to emulate—a role model. With this technique, you will want to:

1. Target an area for action.

2. Identify someone who is already highly successful at this activity.

3. Borrow his/her areas of genius—mentally put yourself into his/her mind and body.

4. See yourself performing the task as your role model would perform it.

5. Perform the activity.

6. Reward yourself with an energy-boosting activity.

To demonstrate this technique, assume that you have been given a career development opportunity to lead an enterprise-wide initiative. Also assume that working across the organization and presenting your recommendations to the management committee is a new experience for you. In this case, your mission is two-fold: You have to successfully lead this initiative AND grow professionally in the process.

When undertaking a role that is new to you, your first step should be to identify one or more people who have already been successful in such a role. You will then need to study the factors, approach, competencies demonstrated, etc., which led to their success. Read about them. Meet with them. Ask them to be your mentor. Do whatever it takes to identify their success criteria. Finally, take what you have learned, blend it with your own persona, and make it your own. You will then need to act and follow through in an appropriate way to complete your assignment.

Routines

Most of us are programmed to use one style or combination of styles to such an extent that the style becomes a habit for us. To break the habit of a particular style, it can be helpful to come up with a new routine.

For example, if you are technically oriented and have been asked to lead the communications work stream for a major reorganization, your natural inclination might be to develop your plans alone. However, you recognize that the success of the change initiative hinges on your team's ability to reach a broad and diverse employee base. You could decide to establish short daily meetings with tight agendas, fixed time commitments, and definitive action steps. When the meetings are over, you can retreat to your office to work on your specific action items. Once a week, you should personally review your progress in adhering to this routine and grade yourself accordingly. If more or less emphasis on communication is needed in the upcoming week, adjust your meeting schedule as appropriate.

In sum, the process for adapting your style through a routine includes six steps:

1. Target an area for action.

2. Break your pattern of thought—imagine yourself as being successful.

3. Undertake the activity when you are fresh and full of energy.

4. Set a schedule that requires you to perform the activity on a regular, repeated basis.

5. Reward yourself with an energy-boosting activity.

6. Create a simple personal scorecard that measures your adherence to performing this routine.

Adapting Leadership Style

Dave was a successful senior executive with a Fortune 100 company. In his illustrious career he had led many of his firm's operating divisions. His career aspiration was to one day sit on the executive committee for his company. However, at his age, his time was running out. In every position he held, Dave always made his numbers and achieved his operating and financial performance objectives. Unfortunately, his abrupt style left a trail of "dead and bleeding bodies" in his wake. The chairman told him that he had one last chance to clean up his act. To do so, Dave turned to an executive coach. Dave listened to his coach's advice and learned to more fully engage his employees at all levels. Instead of criticizing and demeaning those with ideas different than his own, he turned to more mentoring, coaching, and teaching.

On one occasion his coach asked Dave, "I noticed that you are asking your people for their opinions. Why are you doing that?" Dave replied, "I realized that people just want to have a voice. They want to express their opinions. So I let them. In the process, I'm testing myself to make sure I'm not missing anything. Even if I make a decision different than their recommendation, they seem to be okay with that. In fact, as long as they have a voice, they commit to the ultimate direction. Sometimes I am able to share factors that they haven't considered and they seem to appreciate learning what goes into my thinking."

The coach replied, "Dave, this is commendable, yet so far away from your personal leadership style. What caused you to make the change?" Dave answered, "I guess I realized that people really want to be a part of something bigger than themselves and that when they disagree they are not trying to be difficult as much as they want to be sure we come up with the very best solution. At the end of the day, I'm still the boss. I still make the final decisions. Sometimes I change based on people's input and sometimes I don't—but now I always listen."

This example illustrated how one leader adapted his style. His own Passions for Leading and Results helped Dave realize that he needed more of a People Mindset, which in turn helped him adapt and use more of an Influencing/Steady Style in place of his natural Driving Style.

Change at the Core starts with you!

Chapter Highlights

In Chapters 13 and 14, we will look at implementing Change at the Core with your team and sustaining the momentum you've generated by unleashing energy in yourself and in others.

13

Implementing Change at the Core with Your Team

Let's recap. So far, you've learned the four major steps for leading Change at the Core:

1. Understand each person's internal energy.

2. Connect and communicate to promote openness to change.

3. Understand, appreciate, and address resistance.

4. Align and unleash each person's energy to power the change.

You understand that internal energy is the secret ingredient of the Change at the Core process.

You've mastered the three elements of internal energy:

- Style

- Passion

- Mindset

You have even taken a look at your own style, passion, and mindset and are making plans for leveraging your own internal energy.

What Next?

Where do you begin when it comes to applying what you've learned with your own team? In our work we have seen leaders successfully apply Change at the Core using formal, informal, and hybrid approaches.

The Formal Approach

In earlier chapters, you began to form some hypotheses about your team members' internal energy. By nature, the process you used to come to those conclusions is very subjective and dependent on your personal point of view. To get a more accurate picture of a person's Internal energy patterns in our practice, we use a series of scientifically based online assessments that are much more accurate and objective. If you'd like to explore using these assessments with your team, we ask you to use the phone or e-mail information on the last page of this book to contact us.

Engaging an outside consultant is an example of the formal approach to implementing Change at the Core. In the formal approach, a consultant will partner with you to:

1. Have everyone on your team complete assessments to gauge their styles, passions, and mindsets.

2. Bring your team together to share assessment results.

3. Help you implement the four steps of Change at the Core in partnership with individuals on your team.

4. Bring the team together periodically for energizing interactions that focus on aligning, channeling, and unleashing energy in order to help the team as a whole succeed.

The Informal Approach

While we've been a part of many successful change efforts, there are countless other situations where individual leaders have applied what they have learned about internal energy without our direct and personal help. These leaders use a variety of creative approaches, such as giving a copy of this book to each person on their team and then having "book group" discussions about how the team can apply the concepts to their own change projects. Others apply their own awareness of internal energy to initiate conversations with their people about their strengths and what energizes or de-energizes them—without necessarily using a formal assessment or even the names of the styles and passions.

A Hybrid Approach

Lastly, you can experiment with a hybrid approach. In cases like this, you might hire a consultant to help your team understand the concept of internal energy and the elements of style, passion, and mindset. With a shared understanding, you and your team will immediately be able to have meaningful discussions about who can best contribute where and how.

Getting a Glimpse of Energy

We were recently asked to facilitate a two-hour workshop as part of a change team's initial launch. This particular change had been mandated from a parent organization and was so significant that it would take more than 18 months to plan and implement. At this early stage, the team members themselves had not been told the details of the change initiative that they would ultimately be responsible for.

We decided to help the team get started with a positive outlook by introducing the fact that each of them would play a pivotal role and that we hoped they would each bring their strengths to bear on the project. We briefly introduced the concept of Style and asked people to self sort into groups according to the Style that most attracted them. Once each person had joined a group, we asked the teams to discuss and share how they could utilize their natural strengths to the benefit of the change team as a whole. The energy in the room was unbelievable! People were proactively volunteering for roles and looking for partners who would complement their natural styles.

While this team has a lot of work to do over the next year and a half, they have already reported more success than they have experienced in the past.

Key Takeaways

Whether you choose a formal, informal, or hybrid approach, we hope you will find value in remembering these key points:

1. Individual commitment is at the heart of all successful change.

2. For you to generate real commitment from other people, they first have to agree that the change is good for them (based on their passions). Second, they need to consciously wrap their heads around the change initiative and agree to go forward with the proposed approach (mindsets). Finally, they need to activate their hands (styles) to make the change a reality.

3. Commitment is the result of truly connecting, communicating, and collaborating.

"Leadership is leaders inducing followers to act for certain goals that
represent the values and the motivations—the wants and needs,
the aspirations and expectations—of both leaders and followers.
And the genius of leadership lies in the manner in which leaders see
and act on their own and their followers' values and motivations."

~ James McGregor Burns, Author of Leadership

14

Sustaining Change at the Core

At this point you may expect that you should be seeing change all around you. But despite all of your hard work, you aren't done yet.

You may have started a fire, but this is the worst time to abandon your people. After all, you know what they call people who light fires and leave, right? Arsonists![29]

You can implement the steps we discussed and still not see change taking place. People can be all fired up—and go nowhere.

Think about the last time you flew across the country. Your plane landed and taxied to the gate. The second everyone heard that "ding" and the seat belt light went off, what happened? Everyone on airplane jumped up and went nowhere! They felt the urgency—they wanted to get off that plane—but they couldn't do anything about it.

If you want to see real change happen, you have to empower people to make it happen. Now "empower" is one of those words that can mean a lot of different things to different people. When we use it here, we mean giving people what they need in order to take action. If people don't have what they need or if something is in their way, change is not going to happen!

Empowering Your Team

Once you have unleashed the energy at the core of your people, you need to ensure that they are empowered to take action. The reality is that we could devote an entire book to this topic alone. For the sake of time, let's look at just a few of the most essential factors:

Periodic check-ins not only reinforce change, they can also be key to unleashing interactional and group energy.

- Clear expectations

- Access to information

- Authority

- Equipment

- Knowledge, skills, and ability

John Kotter points out that when people are left to fend for themselves, frustration grows and change is undermined.[30] Take a minute or two to think about the changes you'd like to see in your organization. Now put yourself in the shoes of one of your frontline employees. What will he or she need to make that happen? Have you asked?

Reinforcing Change

Ultimately every organizational transformation comes down to changing people's behavior. If you ever raised a pet or a child, then you have experience in changing behavior. Based on your experience, you know that behavior changes don't happen without reinforcement. While the steps you have learned here will help you get started, you also need to be sure to pay attention to reinforcing the change you want to see.

One way to reinforce change is to reconnect with the individuals on your team and your team as a whole. As we discussed in Chapter 13, these periodic check-ins not only reinforce change, they can also be key to unleashing interactional and group energy.

A Few Words on Repetition

When you are in the process of leading change, you are going to have to repeat yourself. A lot.

In our work with organizations, we frequently find ourselves reminding clients of this fact. Since they are accountable for getting people committed, they can easily be frustrated when everyone doesn't get it as fast as they want them to.

If you are introducing a new compensation system, reorganizing your company, or introducing a new product, you've probably been working on this long before you unveil it to the people who are going to need to execute the day-to-day details. William Bridges, a renowned expert on organizational transition, calls this phenomenon the Marathon Effect.[31]

If you have ever run (or watched) a large marathon you know that at the start of the event the best runners are right on the starting line. Where are the first-timers? Way at the back! Think about one of the big races with thousands of runners—like the Marine Corp marathon in Washington, D.C. It can take about an hour for someone at the very back to even get up to the start line. By that time, the ones who were at the front are halfway through the race!

If it's your initiative, your project, by the time you say "let's go" you are thinking that everyone should be right there with you on the starting line. They aren't. They are way at the back and they need time to catch up.

Jack Welch reminds us that we have to be patient. He warns that, "The vision becomes boring to the person who came up with it." It's tempting to keep changing your message—making it flashier, making it new. Don't. To get people on the same page, you can't keep giving them new pages.

When you are in the process of leading change, you are going to have to repeat yourself. A lot.

A Few Words on Rewards

Another aspect of reinforcement has to do with rewards. Upton Sinclair once wrote, "It is difficult to get a man to understand something when his salary depends upon his not understanding it." If you want to sustain change, you have to consider what you are paying people to do.

Think about your organization's reward structures—both the informal and the formal. Which behaviors are getting reinforced and rewarded? The new ones you want to see or the old behaviors you want to do away with? If the answer is "the old behaviors," you most likely need to take on a Systems Mindset and involve the right people in revising expectations and reward structures. Remember the old adage: Only behavior that gets rewarded gets repeated.

Of course, when considering rewards, keep in mind intrinsic rewards as well as extrinsic ones. Our awareness of passions has taught us that different people will find various activities to be rewarding or draining. In addition to your organization's formal reward system, you have a powerful tool for change at work in the heart of every person.

Final Thoughts

Think about the last time you made a campfire. You took steps to prepare the wood and kindling before you lit the match. Once you ignited the spark, you strategically fed fuel to the fire to keep it going.

Organizational change works much the same way. You've got to light a fire inside people, not under them. And you've got to keep feeding the fire if you want it to last.

Ultimately, if you want people to change, you've got to be the spark that lights the fire within them.

You've got to connect with people. You've got to understand and address their concerns. You've got to find a way to power change—not push it or plead for it. You've got to close the change gap. We hope Change at the Core gives you the tools and techniques to do just that.

Endnotes

1   James Kouzes and Barry Posner, *The Leadership Challenge*, 3rd Edition. (San Francisco: Jossey-Bass, 2002), p 177.

2   John Kotter, *A Sense of Urgency* (Boston, MA: Harvard Business School Publishing), p. 13.

3   *IBID*, p. 11.

4   *IBM's Global CEO Study, 2008.*

5   Best practices were developed based on the combined works of John Kotter and Scott Anthony. Anthony's findings were published in his *Harvard Business Review* blog on April 15, 2008. See the John Kotter references above and below for details on his publications.

6   Margaret Wheatley and Deborah Frieze, "Emergence," *Leadership Excellence,* May 2008, p. 10.

7   Connie Hritz, "Change Model," *Leadership Excellence,* May 2008, p. 14.

8   Neslund, Richard, *Energizing Leadership,* Pre-publication Paper, Sept. 2008.

9   "Organizing for Successful Change Management: A McKinsey Global Survey," *The McKinsey Quarterly,* June 2006.

10 Rob Cross, Wayne Baker, and Andrew Parker, "What Creates Energy in Organizations?", *MIT Sloan Management Review*, Summer 2003.

11   *IBID.*

12   Lynda Gratton, *Hot Spots: Why Some Teams, Workplaces, and Organizations Buzz with Energy—And Others Don't* (San Francisco: Berrett-Koehler Publishers, 2007).

13   For more information on the history of the DISC instrument that we use, please see *The Universal Language of DISC—A Reference Manual* by Bill J. Bonnstetter and Judy I. Sutter.

14   Population numbers for the DISC styles provided courtesy of Target Training International.

15   Malcolm Gladwell, *The Tipping Point* (New York: Little, Brown and Company, 2000).

16   John Kotter and Holger Rathgeber, *Our Iceberg is Melting* (New York: Saint Martin's Press, 2005).

17   Eduard Spranger, *Types of Men: The Psychology and Ethics of Personality.* (Halle: Max Niemeyer, 1928). Original work published in 1914.

18   For more information on the Workplace Motivators, see the *Personal Interests, Attitudes and Values Certification and Home Study Guide* by Bill J. Bonnstetter, Randy Jay Widrick and Rick Bowers. Another source is the e-book *If I Knew Then—How to Take Control of Your Career and Build the Lifestyle You Deserve* by Bill J. Bonnstetter.

19   Thomas Herrington and Patrick Malone, "Cracking the Code," *Leadership Excellence,* Feb. 2008, p.14.

20   Judy Rosenblum, Deb Stout, Leah Houde, "Engaging Your People in Your Strategy Through Education," *Duke Corporate Education*, 2003.

21   Peter Block, "Possibilities," *Leadership Excellence*, May 2008, p. 18.

[22] We have learned a great deal from the works of Rick Maurer and John Kotter, who have both written extensively about understanding, appreciating, and addressing resistance.

[23] Rick Maurer, *Why Don't You Want What I Want?* (Austin, Texas: Bard Press, 2002).

[24] Rick Maurer, *Leading from the Middle* (Arlington, Va.: Maurer & Associates, 2008) p. 28.

[25] John Kotter, *A Sense of Urgency* (Boston, MA: Harvard Business School Publishing).

[26] Rick Maurer, *Making a Compelling Case for Middle* (Arlington, Va.: Maurer & Associates, 2004) p. 1.

[27] Bob Rosen, *Just Enough Anxiety* (New York: Penguin Group, 2008).

[28] The referenced works of William Bridges include *Surviving Corporate Transition* (Doubleday, 1988) and *Managing Transitions* (Cambridge, MA: Perseus Books, 1991).

[29] Thanks to David Hyatt for the arsonist humor.

[30] John Kotter and Dan Cohen, *The Heart of Change* (Harvard Business School Press, 2002).

[31] William Bridges, *Managing Transitions* (Cambridge, MA: Perseus Books, 1991).

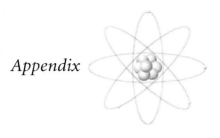

"Just for Fun" Activity Answers

Penguin Styles

Alice—the tough, practical penguin who had a reputation for getting things done fast.   Style: Driving

Louis—the calm and reflective head penguin who could always read the energy of the group.   Style: Steady

Jordan—the logical penguin who often asked intellectual questions and was known as "The Professor."   Style: Careful

Buddy—the penguin that did away with PowerPoint and told a compelling story.   Style: Influencing

Passions and Advertisements

The Few, The Proud, The Marines	Lead, Tradition
Pursuit of Perfection	Lead, Creativity
M'm. M'm. Good	People, Tradition
Learning Together	Knowledge, People
We Bring Good Things to Life	People, Tradition
"Just Win Baby"	Results, Lead

Acknowledgements

First and foremost, we would like to thank our spouses, Steve Mack and Jeannie Radio, for both their support and crucial contributions to the book.

Marshall Goldsmith once wrote, "Feedback is a gift that only others can give you." We would like to express our gratitude to a very special team of friends, family members, and colleagues who took the time to review early drafts and provide us with the gift of honest and constructive feedback: Deanna Banks, Laura Bodenschatz, Alice Buchanan, Rod Johnson, Vinay Kumar, Jennifer McCollum and Beth Radio.

As we discuss in this book, every person on earth has a unique and amazing combination of strengths and talents. We are grateful to have had the support of a team of talented people who brought their strengths to this project: Steffi Ruben for her artistic talent, Amy Mayer for her eagle eye, and Patrice Rhoades-Baum for her brilliance with messaging.

We would also like to thank Felicity Tagliareni, Jim Stryker, and the team of folks at Duke Corporate Education—partners who have taught, challenged, and encouraged us for many years. We are also indebted to Mary Saily, the consummate connector who introduced the two of us many years ago.

The internal energy concept that is central to our Change at the Core approach is grounded in three assessment instruments that have been developed, validated, and refined thanks to the extraordinary work of the team at Target Training International. We thank Jim Robins and Favor Larson for allowing us to be part of their community and enabling us to share these powerful tools with our clients.

In Eastern cultures it is traditional for teachers to give a prayer of thanks to all of the teachers who preceded them before they themselves begin to teach others. In this vein, we would like to thank the mentors and thought leaders who have influenced and guided us. We hope our work honors you—in particular Bill Bonnstetter, Anthony Robbins, Larry Stewart, William Bridges, John Kotter, and Rick Maurer.

About the Authors

Myron J. Radio is the founder and president of The R Group. Myron's specialty is building high-powered teams and developing the people within them. Myron offers a complete range of organizational diagnostics and developmental programs that include meeting facilitation; training; workshops; keynote speeches; and coaching in the areas of change management, strategic and tactical planning, and organizational effectiveness. Myron and his wife Jeannie live in the Washington, D.C., area.

Myron can be reached at:
mradio@the-r-group.com
(703) 476-5575
www.the-r-group.com

Wendy B. Mack is the founder and president of T3 Consulting LLC. Wendy combines her expertise in organizational communication and her hands-on experience with large-scale transformation projects to help leaders engage their employees, align their organizations, and make change happen fast and effectively. Wendy works with change leaders and change teams via keynote speeches, workshops, strategic consulting, and coaching. Wendy and her husband Steve live in Woodland Park, Colorado.

Wendy can be reached at:
wendy@t3consultingllc.com
(719) 687-8561
www.wendymack.com

Ordering Information

To order additional copies of *Change at the Core*, please visit www.ChangeAtTheCore.com or e-mail info@peakpublishing.org.

Printed in the United States
138235LV00001B/2/P